W9-CII-723

The book of
Christmas
Carols

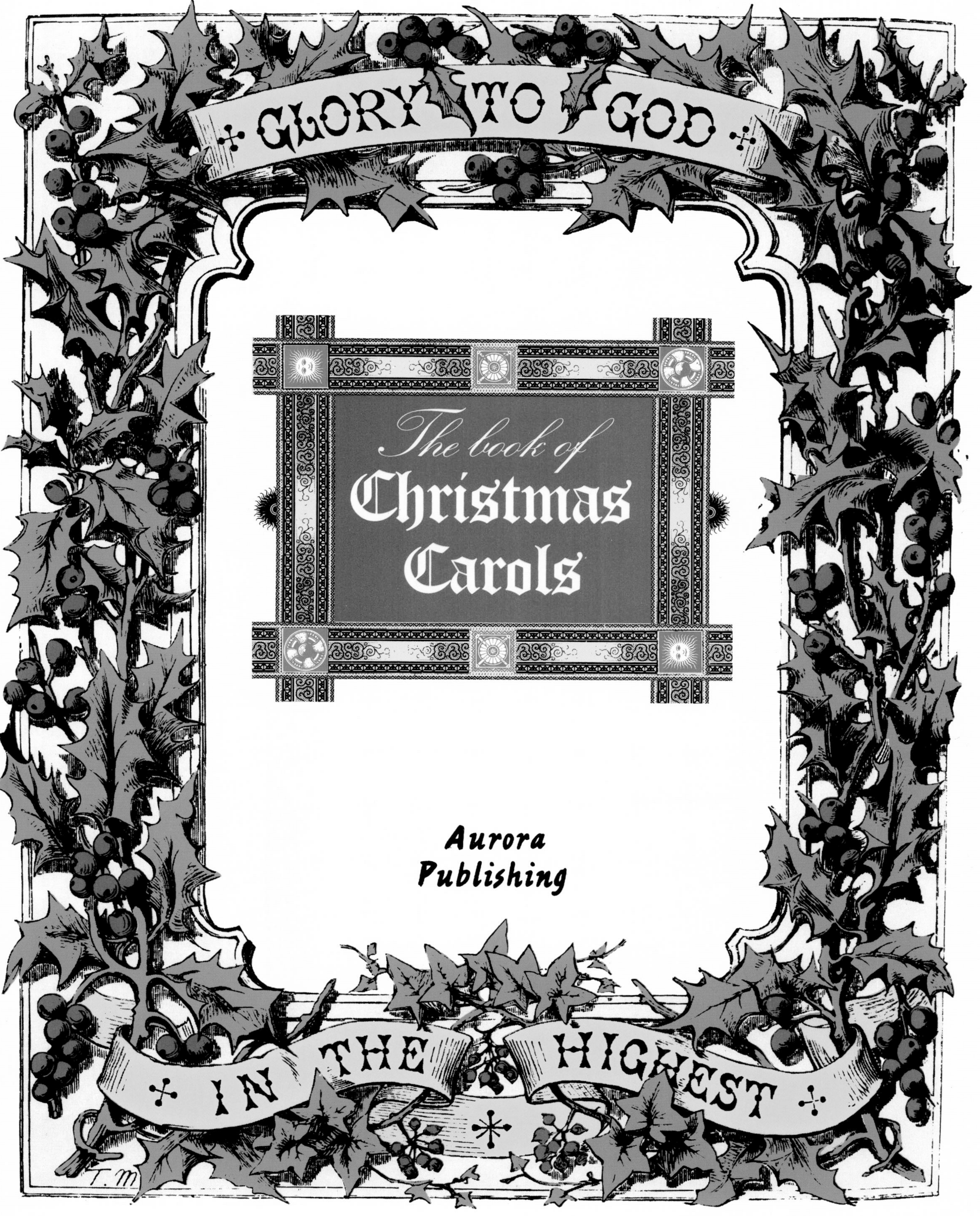
GLORY TO GOD
IN THE HIGHEST
T. M

The book of Christmas Carols

Aurora Publishing

A QUANTUM BOOK

Published by Aurora Publishing
A Division of Aurora Enterprises Ltd
Unit 9, Bradley Fold Trading Estate
Radcliffe Moor Road, Bradley Fold
Bolton BL2 6RT

This edition printed 1996

ISBN 1-85926-072-1

This book was produced by
Quantum Books Ltd
6 Blundell Street
London N7 9BH

Art Director Peter Bridgewater

Typeset in Great Britain by
Central Southern Typesetting, Eastbourne
Colour origination in Hong Kong by
Universal Colour Scanning Limited, Hong Kong
Printed in Singapore by Star Standard Industries Pte. Ltd

CONTENTS

CAROL – the word itself makes us think of rosycheeked choirboys, good food, ceremonies and tradition. It has come to imply joyous singing, not only at Christmas – we speak of birds 'carolling' in the spring. But it has not always had this meaning.

The word itself comes from the old French 'carole', a type of song, almost always in 3/4 time, similar to the English form, and often containing a mixture of languages, such as French, Latin, Basque, and Provençale. In medieval France the carole started as a courtly dancing song, and then gradually spread through the population at large. When the carol reached England in about 1300, it was a popular form which told stories and celebrated religious themes, and was often used to accompany festivals. Carols were still being written in the time of King Henry VIII, in the first half of the 16th century, but by the end of his reign the medieval carol had reached the end of its life. Other types of carol were to take its place.

The English medieval carol retained strong links with its French relation, mainly in the dancelike rhythm of 3-in-a-bar, but in other ways too. The courtly aspect, for instance, is reflected in the survival of the Holly and the Ivy theme – Holly is man, Ivy, woman, a typical image of French chivalrous poetry – and a well-known example of this is *Green Groweth the Holly*, written by Henry VIII himself.

It may seem strange to us today that carols were originally used for dancing, since to dance in church smacks of irreverence. But in the French cathedral of Sens in the 12th century the clergy were permitted to dance so long as their feet did not leave the ground! The Franciscan friars were particularly devoted to singing and dancing, and it may be that they brought the carole and its associated dances to England in the early 13th century.

Up until the reign of Henry VIII there were three main types of carol: the popular, cheerful one for dancing, the more serious one written for purely religious use, and the one written by famous composers for performance by professional choirs of the day. In the reign of Henry, himself a skilful and poet and musician, we can see the themes emerging in carols that we think of today as typical: the merriment of 'Sir Christmas', the lavish banquets typified by the boar's head, the roaring log fires, and the decorations of holly, ivy and mistletoe. The religious side was still important, but the emphasis on enjoyment was gaining a hold.

The definition of a carol is a poem which has a number of verses, interspersed with one or more refrains, or as we should more commonly say today, choruses. A true carol should also have a religious element, even if the carol is not intended for use in church. In fact, carols have served many different purposes. For example, on his return to London in 1415, after his famous victory over the French at Agincourt, Henry V would have been delighted to hear the patriotic carol, *Our King went forth*, celebrating the event in a mixture of English and Latin. One of the two Latin choruses translates as "the English give thanks to God", thus preserving the religious element of the song.

With the coming of the Elizabethan age, in the second half of the 16th century, the carol began to change; the sacred element became more important again. Carols for Christmas and the New Year were written by leading composers like William Byrd to be performed both in the church and at court. We associate the carol almost exclusively with Christmas, but this is a completely modern view. Carols were written for almost any occasion or season; for a celebration (like the Agincourt carol), for making merry at a feast, for singing the praises of the Virgin Mary, for welcoming the spring, and, of course, for celebrating Christ's birth at Christmas. But only in the late 19th century did Christmas take over as the only feast to be celebrated with carols.

During the 17th century many forms of public entertainment came under attack from Oliver Cromwell and the Puritans, who ruled briefly in England from 1649 to 1660. They regarded the merrier forms of music, like the carol, as frivolous, and attempted to suppress them. Solemn carols were approved, and since there are carols for every mood — lullabies, like *Sleep Holy Babe*, melancholy ones, like *The Coventry Carol*, happy ones, like *I Saw Three Ships*, and stirring ones, like *God Rest You Merry, Gentlemen* — the spirit of the carol could not be suppressed completely. With the end of the rule of the Puritans and the restoration of the monarchy in 1660, carols emerged as popular as ever.

From this time onwards carols of the kind that we know and enjoy singing today began to appear. No longer written down as a work of art by composers, the carol began to take on a popular life of its own. Tunes circulated among the people, passed on orally, often with different words and even tunes, from place to place. Carols which crossed to the New World would scarcely be recognizable to those people who still sing their own versions, so different have the words and music become with the passage of time. In England, carols, like ballads, were circulated on broadsheets which cost a penny a time; often they were illustrated with decorative woodcuts. This practice survived, in fact, until the early 20th century, evidence of how genuinely popular a form the carol had become. True, in the early years of the 19th century, its popularity began to wane slightly. By this time a sizeable number of carols, like *God Rest You Merry, Gentlemen*, and *Unto Us a Boy Is Born*, were such an important part of religious life that their survival was not in doubt. But some of the old carols began to be forgotten, and had it not been for the growing interest of a number of historians, like William Hone, who wrote *English Mysteries Described*, they surely would have been lost to later generations.

In the same year that Hone's book was published, Gilbert Davies published *Some Ancient Christmas Carols*, in which he described a typical English West Country Christmas in the late 18th century. "At seven or eight o'clock in the evening cakes were drawn hot from the oven, cyder or beer cheered the spirits in every house, and the singing of carols was continued late into the night. On Christmas day these carols took the place of Psalms in all the churches, especially at afternoon service, the whole congregation joining in."

The picture that this conjures up is very much the cosy, traditional Christmas such as Mr. Pickwick might have enjoyed in Dickens' famous book. Carols have become a central feature of that traditional festivity throughout the Christian world, and the good things that we eat and drink are frequently mentioned in them.

Our wassail-cup is made
Of the rosemary tree,
And so is your beer
Of the best barley.

Wassailers would walk around the countryside from house to house, singing carols and probably drinking far too much at each one; they are the ancestors of our modern carol singers, who are probably unaware of their direct connection with history.

The effect of the work of men like Hone and Davies was to stimulate new interest in carols. Educated people, as opposed to the common folk, began to take an interest in them in about the middle of the 19th century. Some of the older carols, preserved only in oral tradition until then, began to make their appearance in printed collections like *The Little Book of Carols* published in 1846. Despite this, however, the carol continued to decline until Dr. John Stainer (known to the modern age chiefly for his oratorio, *The Crucifixion*) and the Rev. Mr. Bramley published their collection of forty-two Christmas Carols in 1871. This included thirteen traditional tunes, along with a number of rather inferior new ones, and had the immediate effect of reviving interest in carols. True, there were drawbacks; the tunes received rather dull Victorian arrangements which detracted from the liveliness of their melodies and some of the words were modernized in that suet-pudding manner familiar to us from the worst Victorian hymns. But we should be grateful to Stainer and Bramley for setting off what can only be called a carol revival, the fruits of which we enjoy today.

Their initiative was followed up by a new interest in collecting folk songs, marked by the foundation of the Folk Song Society in 1898. The two most famous collectors of folk songs, Cecil Sharp and Ralph Vaughan Williams, joined with Percy Dearmer and Martin Shaw to publish in 1928 what is still the fullest collection of traditional carols, *The Oxford Book of Carols*. By this time the carol revival was in full spate. Composers like Gustav Holst and Peter Warlock were writing new carols to old words, and traditional tunes like *The Holly and the Ivy* were regaining their place in people's affections. Folk melodies, collected from country people, had an enormous influence on composers of the day; and many of those folk songs were, in fact, carols.

Some of the Victorian carols may, as I have implied, be somewhat dull, but many of them possess abiding virtues. What would Christmas be without *The First Nowell* or *Hark the Herald Angels Sing*? There are exceptions to any rule, and many Victorian carols prove it. But the truth is that, part of Christmas though they are, they are, strictly speaking, rarely carols at all – not having a chorus or refrain, they are Christmas hymns, rather than carols. But that is a pedantic objection; the best Christmas songs are all honorary carols and have become an essential part of our celebrations.

The new tradition of the Festival of Nine Lessons and Carols has kept the flame of the carol revival burning, and many contemporary composers now write their own carols; there are jazz carols and rock carols, and carols from a wide range of countries are

popular all over the world. *Silent Night*, from Austria, is one of the world's most popular carols, and *The Little Drummer Boy* from France, is sung from Europe to America and to the Antipodes.

The carols in this book include most of the several types that I have mentioned, from the oldest to the relatively new. *The Coventry Carol*, one of the loveliest lullabies ever written, comes from the 14th-century mystery play of the Coventry Guild of Tailors and Shearmen. In the play, it is sung just before Herod's soldiers arrive for the slaughter of the Innocents. Christ's birth itself is beautifully described in *Once in Royal David's City*, perhaps the most popular of all the Victorian Christmas carols; the simplicity of the words by Mrs. Alexander are perfectly matched by Gauntlett's melody. To survive the test of time a carol must have just these qualities: simplicity and melodiousness. These are just the qualities possessed by *God Rest You Merry, Gentlemen*, one of the 18th century broadsheet carols, and it retained its popularity during the 19th-century decline of the carol because of them. *The Holy Well* is probably one of the loveliest melodies to any carol; it was written down by Frank Sidgwick. *The Cherry Tree Carol* occurs in many versions, and was one of the most popular of the broadsheet carols.

Carols represent perhaps the most varied and enjoyable of all Western musical forms. Explore them, enjoy them and, most important of all, sing them, and you will share the heritage of simple people who have expressed their devotion through song down the ages.

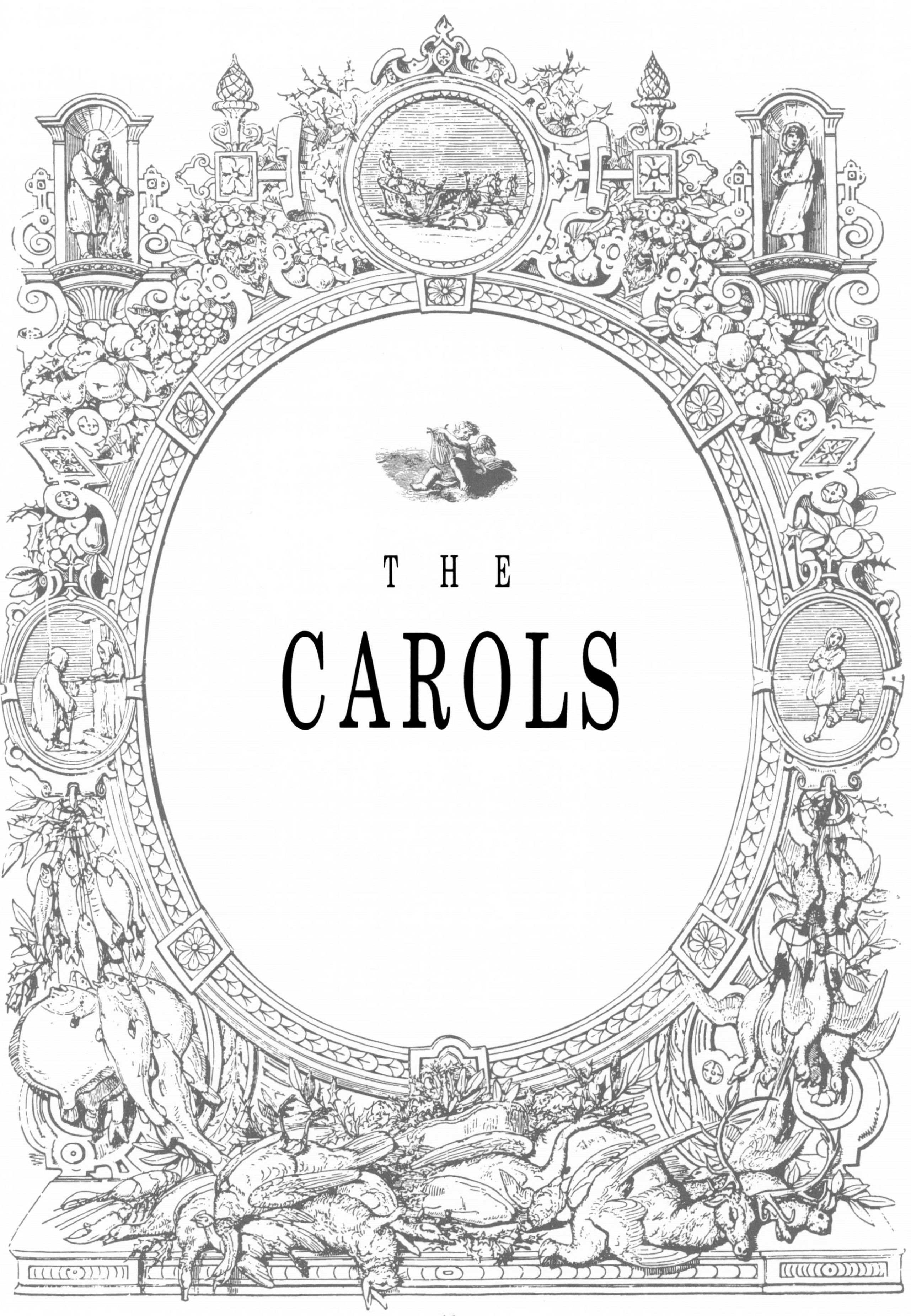

THE CAROLS

ON CHRISTMAS NIGHT

Moderato.
f

mf
On Christ-mas night true Christians sing, To hear what news the
mf

An - gels bring; News of great joy, cause of great mirth, Good

tid - ings of the Saviour's birth, Good tid - ings of the

Sa-viour's birth.
f

2

Angels with joy sing in the air,
No music may with theirs compare;
While prisoners in their chains rejoice
To hear the echos of that voice.
So how on earth can men be sad,
When Jesus comes to make us glad;
From sin and hell to set us free,
And buy for us our liberty?

3

Let sin depart, while we His grace,
And glory see in Jesus' face;
For so shall we sure comforts find
When thus this day we bear in mind.
And from the darkness we have light,
Which makes the Angels sing this night:
"Glory to God, His peace to men,
Both now and evermore." Amen.

mf
The King of kings to us is given, The Lord of earth and
mf
King of heaven; An-gels and men with joy may sing, To
see and bless this newborn King, To see and bless this newborn King.
f

HARK! THE HERALD ANGELS SING

Hark! the He-rald An-gels sing Glo-ry to the New-born King,

Peace on earth and mer-cy mild, God and sin-ners re-con-ciled.

Joy-ful, all ye na-tions, rise, Join the tri-umph of the skies;

With th'An-gel-ic Host pro-claim Christ is born in Beth-le-hem.

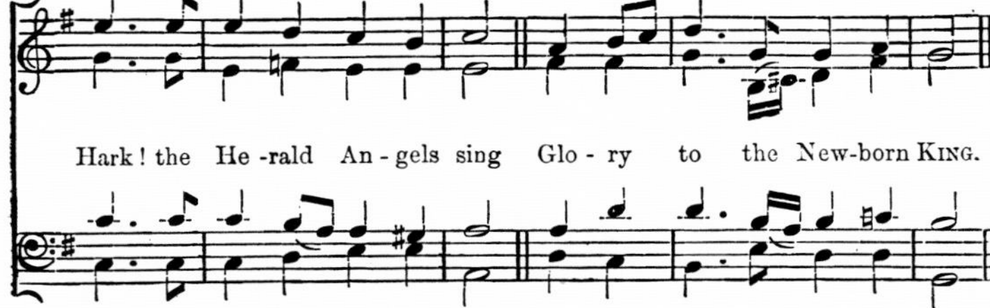
Hark! the He-rald An-gels sing Glo-ry to the New-born King.

— 2 —

CHRIST, by highest Heaven adored,
CHRIST, the Everlasting Lord,
Late in time behold Him come,
Offspring of a Virgin's womb.
Veiled in flesh the Godhead see;
Hail, the Incarnate Deity!
Pleased as Man with man to dwell,
Jesus, our Emmanuel.
Hark! the Herald Angels sing
Glory to the New-born King.

— 3 —

Hail, the Heaven-born Prince of Peace,
Hail, the Sun of Righteousness!
Light and life to all He brings,
Risen with healing in His Wings.
Now He lays His Glory by,
Born that man no more may die,
Born to raise the sons of earth,
Born to give them Second Birth.
Hark! the Herald Angels sing
Glory to the New-born King.

A HAPPY CHRISTMAS

SILENT NIGHT

1. Si - lent night, Ho - ly night, All is calm, all is bright;

'Round yon vir - gin mo - ther and Child, Ho - ly In - fant so tender and mild,

Sleep in heavenly peace, Sleep in heavenly peace.

2

Silent night, Holy night,
Shepherds quake at the sight;
Glories stream from heaven afar,
Heav'nly hosts sing Alleluia!
Christ the Saviour is born!
Christ the Saviour is born!

3

Silent night, Holy night,
Son of God, love's pure light;
Radiance beams from Thy holy face,
With the dawn of redeeming grace,
Jesus, Lord, at thy birth,
Jesus, Lord, at thy birth.

Wishes

THE BABE OF BETHLEHEM

p
The Babe in Beth - lem's man - ger laid,

In hum - ble form so low; By wond'-ring an - gels

is surveyed Through all His scenes of woe.

ff Chorus.
No - el, No - el, ... Now

2

A Saviour! sinners all around
Sing, shout the wondrous word;
Let every bosom hail the sound,
A Saviour! Christ the Lord
Noel, Noel, &c.

3

For not to sit on David's throne
With worldly pomp and joy,
He came for sinners to atone,
And Satan to destroy.
Noel, Noel, &c.

4

To preach the Word of Life Divine,
And feed with living Bread,
To heal the sick with hand benign,
And raise to life the dead.
Noel, Noel, &c.

5

He preached, He suffered, bled and died,
Uplift 'twixt earth and skies;
In sinners' stead was crucified,
For sin a sacrifice.
Noel, Noel, &c.

6

Well may we sing a Saviour's birth,
Who need the grace so given,
And hail His coming down to earth,
Who raises us to Heaven.
Noel, Noel, &c.

birth
sing a Saviour's birth, All hail, all hail, His com - ing
birth

down to earth, Who rais - es us to Heaven!

Noel
With love and best wishes from me and from mine.

ALL THIS NIGHT

Moderato.
mf
All this night bright an - gels sing, Nev - er was such
mf

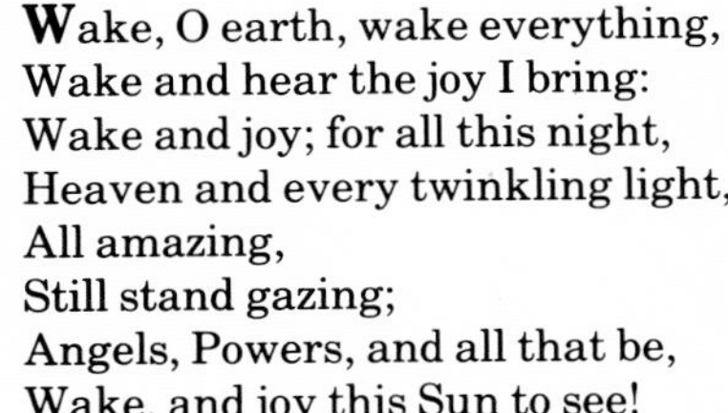

— 2 —

Wake, O earth, wake everything,
Wake and hear the joy I bring:
Wake and joy; for all this night,
Heaven and every twinkling light,
All amazing,
Still stand gazing;
Angels, Powers, and all that be,
Wake, and joy this Sun to see!

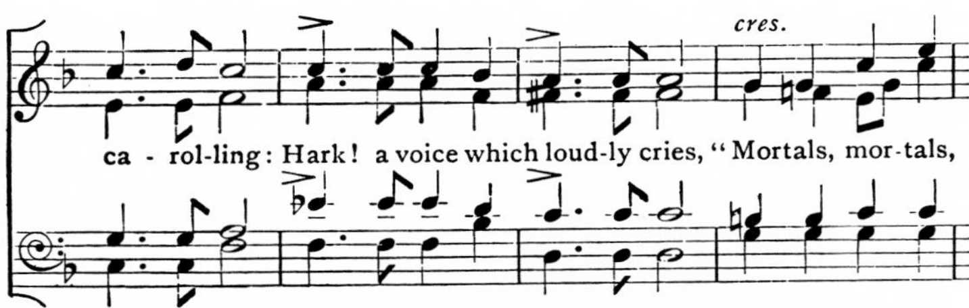
cres.
ca - rol-ling: Hark! a voice which loud-ly cries, "Mortals, mor-tals,

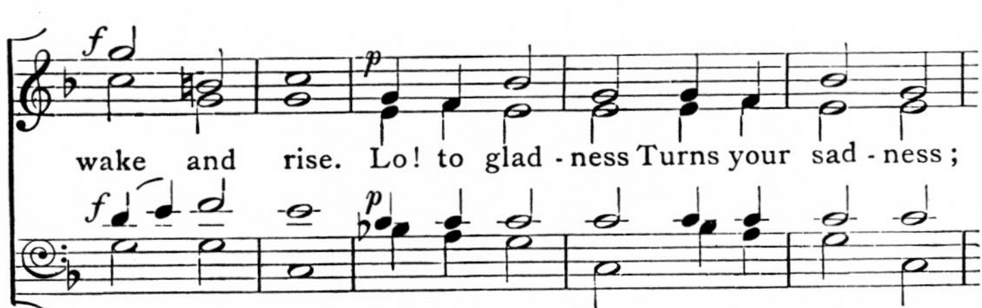
f
p
wake and rise. Lo! to glad - ness Turns your sad - ness;
f
p

cres.
f
From the earth is ris'n a Sun, Shines all night, though day . . be done."
day be
f

VERSE 3.
p
Hail! O Sun, O bless-ed Light, Sent in - to this world by night;
p
mf
dim.
Let Thy rays and heav'n - ly pow'rs Shine in these dark
mf
pp
cres.
souls of ours. For, most du - ly, Thou art tru - ly
pp

f
rall.
ff
God and man, we do con-fess; Hail, O Sun of Right-eous - ness!
f
ff

THE CHRISTMAS CELEBRATION

"Now to God on high be glo - ry, And to

men on earth be peace." 'Tis the Eu - char - ist - ic

an - them, Mu - sic that shall nev - er cease, To a

ran-som'd world pro-claim-ing Je - su's ad-vent, men's re-lease.

— 2 —

Christendom at all her Altars
Once again the tale doth tell
Of His Birth, Who came to vanquish
Sin and Satan, Death and Hell,
Virgin-born, and Manger-cradled,
Jesus our Emmanuel.

— 3 —

See the shepherds, heaven-greeted,
Worship, while the Angels sing;
See the Magi, star-directed,
Their most costly treasures bring;
See earth's simple ones and wise ones
Bending o'er their Baby-King.

— 4 —

Happy Mother, ever Virgin,
Mary clasps Him to her breast,
All succeeding generations
Speaking of her call her blest,
And Saint Joseph joins with wonder
In the homage of the rest.

— 5 —

Now, dear Lord, Thy Birth-day keeping,
As we bend before the shrine,
Find Thee life and health bestowing
Veiled beneath the Bread and Wine.
Make us like Thee, child-like, God-like,
Keep, O keep us ever Thine.

A·MERRY·CHRISTMAS

O COME ALL YE FAITHFUL

Moderato
mf O come, all ye faith - ful, Joy - ful and tri - um - phant, O

come_ ye, O come_ ye to Beth - - le - hem;

Come and_ be - hold_ Him, Born the King of An - gels;

REFRAIN
p O come let us a - dore Him, O come let us a - dore Him, O

come let us a - dore_ Him,_ Christ_ the Lord.

— 2 —

God of God, Light of light,
Lo! He abhors not the Virgin's womb;
Very God, Begotten, not created:
O come let us adore, &c.

— 3 —

Sing, choirs of Angels, Sing in exultation,
Sing, all ye citizens of heaven above;
Glory to God In the highest:
O come let us adore, &c.

— 4 —

Yea, Lord, we greet Thee,
Born this happy morning,
Jesu, to Thee be glory given;
Word of the Father, Now in flesh
appearing:
O come let us adore, &c.

COME ALL YE
FAITHFUL

HE ANGEL GABRIEL

mf
The An-gel Ga-bri-el from God Was sent to
mf

Ga - li-lee, Un-to a Vir-gin fair and free, Whose name was

call'd Ma-ry. And when the An-gel thi-ther came, He

fell down on his knee, And look-ing in the

Vir - gin's face, Said "Hail, all hail, Ma - ry!"

— 2 —

Mary anon looked him upon,
And said, "Sir, what are ye?
I marvel much at tidings such
As thou has brought to me:
Married I am to an old man,
So fell the lot to me;
Therefore, I pray, depart away;
I stand in doubt of thee.
Then sing we, &c.

— 3 —

"Mary," he said, "be not afraid,
But now believe in me:
The power of God the Holy Ghost
Shall overshadow thee.
Thou shalt conceive, but not to grieve
As the Lord told unto me;
God's own dear Son from heaven shall come
And shall be born of thee."
Then sing we, &c.

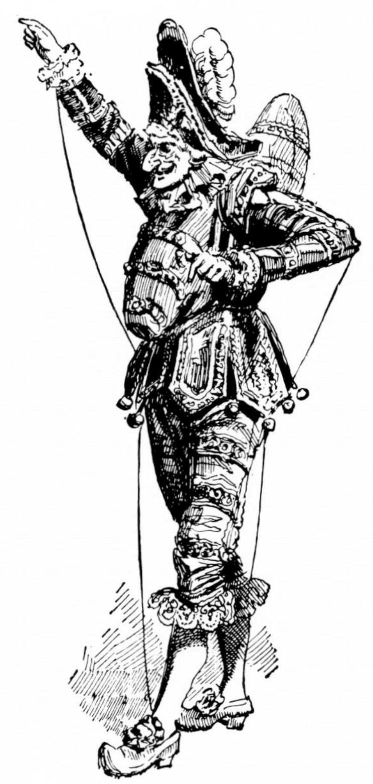

CHORUS.
Then sing we all, both great and small, No - el, No - el, No - el; We may re - joice to hear the voice Of An - gel Ga - bri - el.

4

This came to pass as God's will was,
Even as the Angel told.
About midnight an Angel bright
Came to the shepherds' fold,
And told them then both where and when
Born was the Child, our Lord;
And all along this was their song:
"All glory be to God."

Then sing we, &c.

5

Good people all, both great and small,
The which do hear my voice,
With one accord let's praise the Lord,
And in our hearts rejoice;
In love abound to all around,
While we our life-time spend,
While we have space let's pray for grace:
So let my carol end.

Then sing we, &c.

IN BETHLEHEM, THAT NOBLE PLACE

mf
In Beth - le - hem, that no - ble place, As
mf

cres.
f
by the Pro - phet said it was, Of the Vir - gin
f

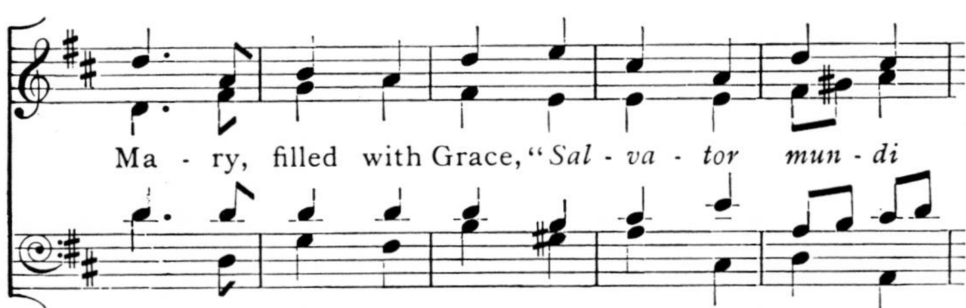

Ma - ry, filled with Grace, "Sal - va - tor mun - di

ff CHORUS.
na - tus est." Be we mer - ry in this
ff

Feast, "In quo Sal - va - tor na - tus est."

— 2 —

On Christmas night an Angel told
The shepherds watching by their fold,
In Bethlehem, full nigh the wold,
"Salvator mundi natus est."
Be we merry, &c.

— 3 —

The shepherds were encompassed right,
About them shone a glorious light,
"Dread ye naught," said the Angel bright,
"Salvator mundi natus est."
Be we merry, &c.

— 4 —

"No cause have ye to be afraid,
For why? this day is Jesus laid
On Mary's lap, that gentle maid:"
"Salvator mundi natus est."
Be we merry, &c.

— 5 —

"And thus in faith find Him ye shall
Laid poorly in an ox's stall."
The shepherds then lauded God all
Quia Salvator natus est.
Be we merry, &c.

A CHILD THIS DAY IS BORN
mf
A Child this day is born, A
Child of high re - nown; Most wor - thy of a
scep - tre, A scep - tre and a crown.
Chorus.
Glad tid - ings to all men, Glad
tid - ings sing we may, Be - cause the King of
kings . . . . . Was born on Christ - mas - Day.
2
These tidings shepherds heard
Whilst watching o'er their fold;
'Twas by an Angel unto them
That night revealed and told.
Glad tidings, &c.
3
Then was there with the Angel
An host incontinent
Of heavenly bright soldiers,
All from the highest sent.
Glad tidings, &c.
4
They praised the Lord our God,
And our celestial King;
All glory be in Paradise,
This heavenly host do sing.
Glad tidings, &c.
5
All glory be to God,
That sitteth still on high,
With praises and with triumph great,
And joyful melody.
Glad tidings, &c.

RAPHAEL TUCK & SONS' "CHRISTMAS" POSTCARD SERIES 1732 Chromographed in Prussia.
A JOYFUL
CHRISTMAS

THE LORD AT FIRST

mf The Lord at first had Ad - am made Out

of the dust and clay, And in his nos - trils

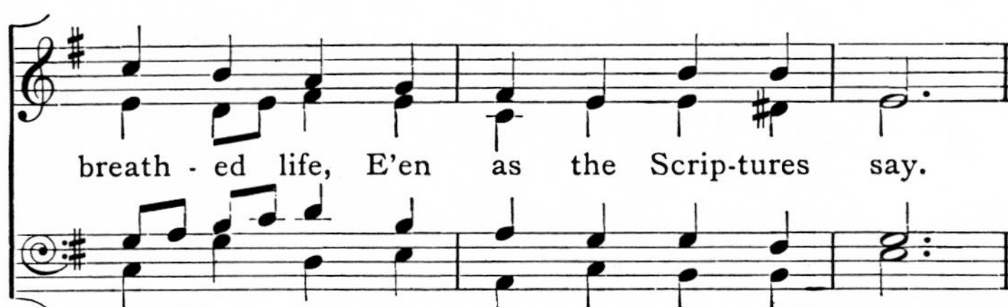
breath - ed life, E'en as the Scrip-tures say.

p And then in E-den's Pa-ra-dise He pla-ced him to dwell, That

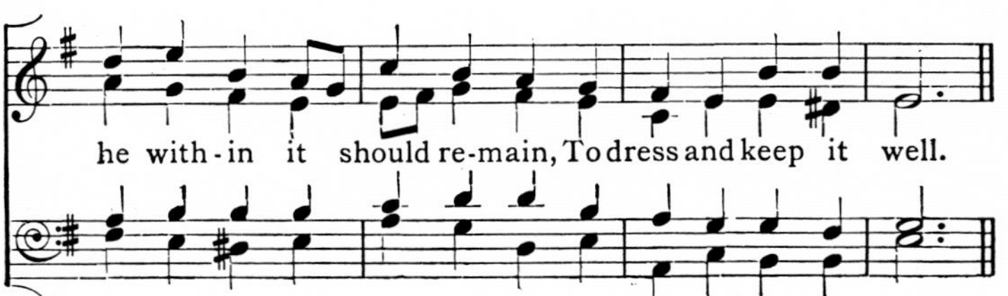
he with-in it should re-main, To dress and keep it well.

— 2 —

And thus within the garden he
Was set, therein to stay;
And in commandment unto him
These words the Lord did say:
"The fruit which in the garden grows
To thee shall be for meat,
Except the tree in midst thereof,
Of which thou shalt not eat."
Now let good Christians, &c.

— 3 —

"For in the day thou shalt it touch
Or dost to it come nigh,
If so thou do but eat thereof,
Then thou shalt surely die."
But Adam he did take no heed
Unto that only thing,
But did transgress God's holy Law,
And so was wrapt in sin.
Now let good Christians, &c.

— 4 —

Now mark the goodness of the Lord,
Which He to mankind bore;
His mercy soon He did extend,
Lost man for to restore:
And therefore to redeem our souls
From death and hell and thrall,
He said His own dear Son should be
The Saviour of us all.
Now let good Christians, &c.

— 5 —

Which promise now is brought to pass:
Christians, believe it well:
And by the death of God's dear Son,
We are redeemed from Hell.
So if we truly do believe,
And do the thing that's right,
Then by His merits we at last
Shall live in Heaven bright.
Then let good Christians, &c.

CHORUS.
ff Now let good Christians all Be-gin A ho-lier life to
live, And to re-joice and mer-ry be, For this is Christmas Eve.

— 6 —

And now the tide is nigh at hand,
In which our Saviour came;
Let us rejoice and merry be
In keeping of the same;
Let's feed the poor and hungry souls,
And such as do it crave;
And when we die, in heaven we
Our sure reward shall have.
Then let good Christians, &c.

JESUS IN THE MANGER

Con spirito.
Why, Most High-est, art Thou ly - ing In a

man-ger poor and low? Thou, the fires of heav'n sup -

- ply - ing, Come a . . sta - ble's cold to know?

TREBLE. CHORUS.
O what works of love stu - pen - dous,
ALTO.
O what works of love stu - pen - dous,
TENOR.
O what works of love stu - pen - dous,
O what works of love stu - pen - dous, Je - su,
1ST BASS.
2ND BASS.
O what works of love stu - pen - dous,
ACCOMP.

— 2 —

On a Mother's breast Thou sleepest,
Mother, yet a Virgin still:
Sad, with eyes bedimmed Thou weepest,
Eyes, which Heaven with gladness fill.
O what works, &c.

— 3 —

Weak the strong, of strength the Giver:
Small, Whose arms creation span;
Bound, Who only can deliver;
Born is He Who ne'er began.
O what works, &c.

f
Were sal - va - tion's price! Burn-ing wert Thou to be -
f
Were sal - va - tion's price! Burn-ing wert Thou to be -
f
Were sal - va - tion's price! Burn - ing wert Thou to be -
(1 & 2.)
Were sal - va - tion's price! Burn-ing wert Thou to be -
f
- friend us, Ex - iles far from Pa - ra - dise.
- friend us, Ex - iles far from Pa - ra - dise.
- friend us, Ex - iles far from Pa - ra - dise.
- friend us, Ex - iles far from Pa - ra - dise.

ARISE, AND HAIL THE SACRED DAY

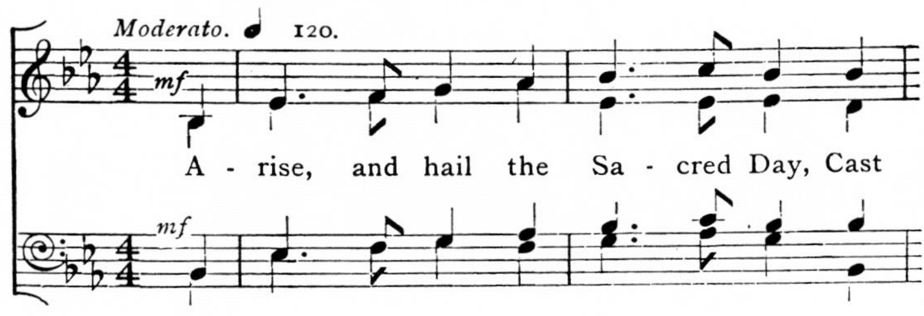
Moderato. ♩ 120.
mf
A - rise, and hail the Sa - cred Day, Cast
mf

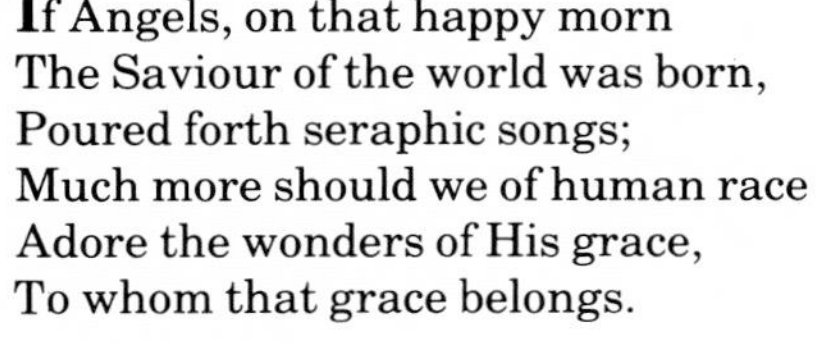

— 2 —

If Angels, on that happy morn
The Saviour of the world was born,
Poured forth seraphic songs;
Much more should we of human race
Adore the wonders of His grace,
To whom that grace belongs.

all low cares of life a-way, And thoughts of mean- er

— 3 —

How wonderful, how vast His love,
Who left the shining realms above,
Those happy seats of rest;
How much for lost mankind He bore,
Their peace and pardon to restore,
Can never be exprest.

f
things; This day to cure our dead ly woes, The
f

— 4 —

While we adore His boundless grace,
And pious joy and mirth take place
Of sorrow, grief, and pain,
Give glory to our God on high,
And not among the general joy
Forget good-will to men.

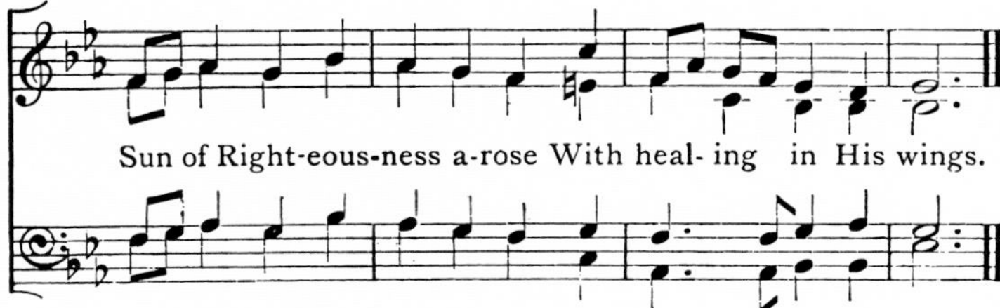
Sun of Right-eous-ness a-rose With heal- ing in His wings.

— 5 —

O then let Heaven and earth rejoice,
Creation's whole united voice,
And hymn the Sacred Day,
When sin and Satan vanquished fell,
And all the powers of death and hell,
Before His sovereign sway.

STAR

Hearty Christmas Greetings

JACOB'S LADDER

As Ja - cob with tra - vel was wea - ry one
day, At night on a stone for a pil - low he
lay, He saw in a vi - sion a lad - der so high, That its
foot was on earth, and its top in the sky.

— 2 —

This ladder is long, it is strong and well-made,
Has stood hundreds of years and is not yet decayed;
Many millions have climbed it and reached Sion's hill,
And thousands by faith are climbing it still.
Hallelujah to Jesus, &c

— 3 —

Come let us ascend: all may climb it who will;
For the Angels of Jacob are guarding it still:
And remember each step, that by faith we pass o'er,
Some Prophet or Martyr hath trod it before.
Hallelujah to Jesus, &c

— 4 —

And when we arrive at the haven of rest
We shall hear the glad words, "Come up hither, ye blest,
Here are regions of light, here are mansions of bliss:"
O, who would not climb such a ladder as this?
Hallelujah to Jesus, &c.

CHORUS.
Hal - le - lu - jah to Je - sus, who died on the
tree, And hath rais'd up a lad - der of mer - cy for
me, And hath rais'd up a lad - der of mer - cy for me.

IN THE COUNTRY NIGH TO BETHLEHEM

In the country nigh to Bethlehem, On a star - ry night of old,

There were in the fields a-bid-ing, Shepherds with their flocks in fold.

Round the flocks the faithful shepherds Kept their watch from eve till morn,

Lest their sheep, so weak and helpless, Should by e - vil beasts be torn.

— 2 —

Haply, through their long night-watches,
They made hill and valley ring
With the songs of holy gladness
Which King David used to sing.
Songs of praise to God their Shepherd,
Who defended them from ill,
And their weary, wandering footsteps
Guided to the waters still.

— 3 —

As they watched, a burst of glory
Shone around them from above,
And a mighty glorious Angel
Calmed their fears with words of love:
"Fear not, for behold I bring you
Tidings full of greatest joy,
Joy eternal, full of gladness,
Joy which nothing can destroy.

— 4 —

"Unto you in David's city,
As was told by Prophet's word,
Christ is born, your God and Saviour,
Christ is born, your King and Lord."
Suddenly a host of Angels
Raised their voices high and sang,
Till the vaulted arch of Heaven
With the echoing chorus rang:

— 5 —

"Glory, glory, in the highest,
Unto God, and peace on earth;
To all nations joyful bring we
Tidings glad of Jesus' birth."
Lift we now our hearts and voices,
Join we all the cheerful cry,
Learned by shepherds from the Angels:
"Glory be to God on high!"

THE STAR IN THE EAST.
The Lord
of Christmas
be with thee.
"When they saw
the star, they
rejoiced with
exceeding great
joy."
Matt. II.10.

THE INCARNATION

Vivace.
mf
The great God of Hea-ven is come down to earth, His

Mo-ther a.. Vir-gin, and sin-less His Birth; The

Fa-ther e-ter-nal His Fa-ther a-lone: He

sleeps in the man-ger; He reigns on the Throne.

— 2 —

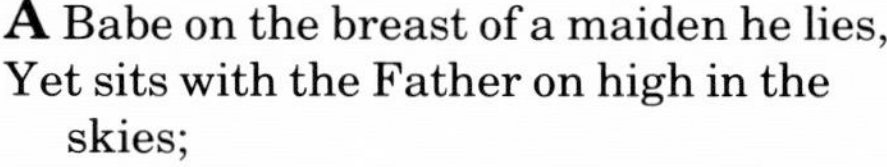

A Babe on the breast of a maiden he lies,
Yet sits with the Father on high in the skies;
Before Him their faces the Seraphim hide,
While Joseph stands waiting, unscared, by His side.
Then let us adore him, &c.

— 3 —

Lo! her is Immanuel, here is the Child,
The Son that was promised to Mary so mild;
Whose power and dominion shall ever increase,
The Prince that shall rule o'er a kingdom of peace.
Then let us adore Him, &c.

— 4 —

The Wonderful Counsellor, boundless in might,
The Father's own Image, the Beam of His Light;
Behold Him now wearing the likeness of man,
Weak, helpless, and speechless, in measure a span,
Then let us adore Him, &c.

ff Chorus.
Then let us a - dore Him, and praise His great love, To
ff
save us poor sin - ners He came from a - bove.

— 5 —

O wonder of wonders, which none can
unfold;
The Ancient of days is an hour or two old;
The Maker of all things is made of the
earth,
Man is worshipped by angels, and God
comes to birth.
Then let us adore Him, &c.

— 6 —

The Word in the bliss of the Godhead
remains,
Yet in Flesh comes to suffer the keenest of
pains;
He is that He was, and for ever shall be,
But becomes that He was not, for you and
for me.
Then let us adore Him, &c.

Love from
Nellie

A Holy Happy Christmas.

See Amid the Winter's Snow

Moderato.
See a-mid the win-ter's snow,
Moderato.
p
Born for us on earth be-low, See the ten-der
Lamb ap-pears, Pro-mised from e-ter-nal years.

— 2 —

Lo, within a manger lies
He who built the starry skies;
He, who throned in height sublime,
Sits amid the Cherubim!
Hail, thou ever-blessed, &c.

— 3 —

Say, ye holy Shepherds, say,
What your joyful news to-day;
Wherefore have ye left your sheep?
On the lonely mountain steep?
Hail, thou ever-blessed, &c.

— 4 —

"**A**s we watched at dead of night,
Lo, we saw a wondrous light;
Angels singing peace on earth,
Told us of a Saviour's Birth."
Hail, thou ever-blessed, &c.

— 5 —

Sacred Infant, all Divine,
What a tender love was Thine;
Thus to come from highest bliss
Down to such a world as this!
Hail, thou ever-blessed, &c.

— 6 —

Teach, O teach us, Holy Child,
By Thy face so meek and mild,
Teach us to resemble Thee,
In Thy sweet humility!
Hail, thou ever-blessed, &c.

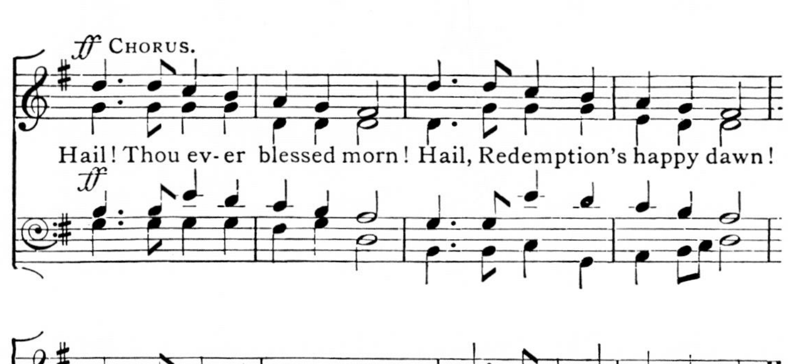
ff Chorus.
Hail! Thou ev-er blessed morn! Hail, Redemption's happy dawn!
ff

Sing thro' all Je - ru - sa - lem, Christ is born in Beth - le - hem.

SAW THREE SHIPS

Briskly.
mf
I saw three ships come sail - ing in, On
mf

Christ-mas day, on Christ-mas day; I saw three ships come

sail - ing in, On Christ-mas day in the morn - ing,

Or this (in 3 parts).
mf
I saw three ships come sail - ing in, On
mf

Christ-mas day, on Christ-mas day; I saw three ships come

sail - ing in, On Christ-mas day in the morn - ing.

2

And what was in those ships all three,
On Christmas day, on Christmas day;
And what was in those ships all three,
On Christmas day in the morning?

3

The Virgin Mary and Christ were there;
On Christmas day, on Christmas day;
The Virgin Mary and Christ were there,
On Christmas day in the morning.

4

Pray, whither sailed those ships all three,
On Christmas day, on Christmas day;
Pray, whither sailed those ships all three,
On Christmas day in the morning?

5

O they sailed into Bethlehem,
On Christmas day, on Christmas day;
O they sailed into Bethlehem,
On Christmas day in the morning.

6

And all the bells on earth shall ring,
On Christmas day, on Christmas day;
And all the bells on earth shall ring,
On Christmas day in the morning.

7

And all the Angels in Heaven shall sing,
On Christmas day, on Christmas day;
And all the Angels in Heaven shall sing,
On Christmas day in the morning.

— 8 —

And all the souls on earth shall sing,
On Christmas day, on Christmas day;
And all the souls on earth shall sing,
On Christmas day in the morning.

— 9 —

Then let us all rejoice amain,
On Christmas day, on Christmas day;
Then let us all rejoice amain,
On Christmas day in the morning.

GOOD KING WENCESLAS

f
Good King Wences-las look'd out On the Feast of Ste - phen,
When the snow lay round a-bout, Deep, and crisp, and e - ven:
Bright - ly shone the moon that night, Though the frost was cru - el,
When a poor man came in sight, Ga-th'ring winter fu - - el.

— 2 —

"Hither, page, and stand by me,
If thou know'st it, telling,
Yonder peasant, who is he?
Where and what his dwelling?
Treble Solo.
"Sire, he lives a good league hence,
Underneath the mountain;
Right against the forest fence,
By Saint Agnes' fountain."

— 3 —

"Bring me flesh, and bring me wine,
Bring me pine-logs hither;
Thou and I will see him dine,
When we bear them thither."
Chorus.
Page and monarch forth they went,
Forth they went together;
Through the rude wind's wild lament,
And the bitter weather.

— 4 —

"Sire, the night is darker now,
And the wind blows stronger;
Fails my heart, I know not how,
I can go no longer."
Tenor Solo.
"Mark my footsteps, good my page!
Tread thou in them boldly:
Thou shalt find the winter's rage
Freeze thy blood less coldly."

— 5 —

In his master's steps he trod,
Where the snow lay dinted;
Heat was in the very sod
Which the saint had printed.
Therefore, Christian men, be sure,
Wealth or rank possessing,
Ye who now will bless the poor,
Shall yourselves find blessing.

THE HOLY WELL

mf
As it fell out one May morning, On one bright ho-li-day, Sweet
mf

Je-sus ask'd of His dear mother, If He might go to play. "To

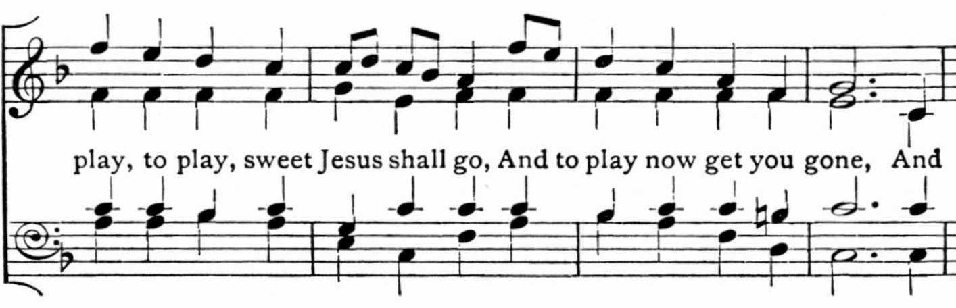
play, to play, sweet Jesus shall go, And to play now get you gone, And

let me hear of no com-plaint At night when you come home."

— 2 —

Sweet Jesus went down to yonder town,
As far as the Holy Well,
And there did see as fine children
As any tongue can tell.
He said "God bless you every one,
May Christ your portion be;
Little children, shall I play with you?
And you shall play with me."

— 3 —

But they made answer to Him, "No,"
They were lords' and ladies' sons;
And He, the meanest of them all,
Was born in an ox's stall.
Sweet Jesus turnèd Him around,
And He neither laughed nor smil'd,
But tears came trickling from His eyes,
Like water from the skies.

— 4 —

Sweet Jesus turnèd Him about,
To His mother's dear home went He,
And said "I've been in yonder town,
As after you may see.
Yea, I have been in yonder town,
As far as the Holy Well;
There did I meet as fine children
As any tongues can tell.

— 5 —

"I bid God bless them ev'ry one,
And Christ their portion be;
Little children, shall I play with you?
And you shall play with me.
But they made answer to me, 'No,'
They were lords' and ladies' sons;
And I, the meanest of them all,
Was born in an ox's stall."

— 6 —

"**T**hough Thou art but a maiden's Child,
Born in an ox's stall,
Thou art the Christ, the King of Heav'n,
The Saviour of them all.
Sweet Jesus, go down to yonder town,
As far as the Holy Well,
And take away those sinful souls,
And dip them deep in hell."

— 7 —

"**N**ay, nay," sweet Jesus mildly said,
"Nay, nay, that must not be,
There are too many sinful souls
Crying out for the help of Me."
Then spake the Angel Gabriel,
"Upon a good set steven.
Although Thou'rt but a maiden's Child,
Thou art the King of Heav'n."

We·have·seen·his Star·in·the·East.

GOOD CHRISTIAN MEN, REJOICE

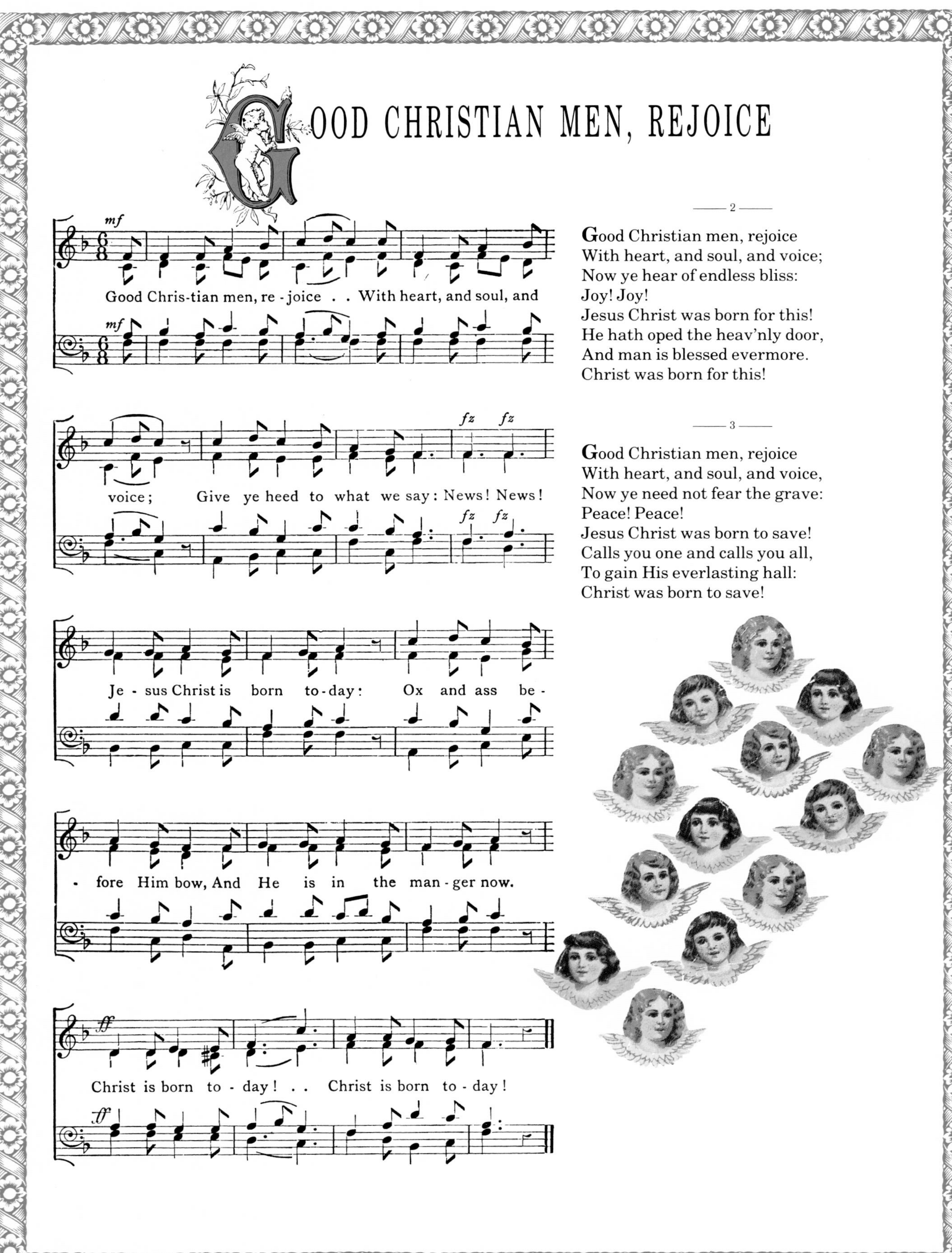
mf
Good Chris-tian men, re - joice . . With heart, and soul, and
voice; Give ye heed to what we say: News! News!
fz fz
Je - sus Christ is born to-day: Ox and ass be -
- fore Him bow, And He is in the man - ger now.
ff
Christ is born to - day! . . Christ is born to - day!

— 2 —

Good Christian men, rejoice
With heart, and soul, and voice;
Now ye hear of endless bliss:
Joy! Joy!
Jesus Christ was born for this!
He hath oped the heav'nly door,
And man is blessed evermore.
Christ was born for this!

— 3 —

Good Christian men, rejoice
With heart, and soul, and voice,
Now ye need not fear the grave:
Peace! Peace!
Jesus Christ was born to save!
Calls you one and calls you all,
To gain His everlasting hall:
Christ was born to save!

GOD REST YOU MERRY, GENTLEMEN

mf
God rest you mer-ry, gen-tle-men, Let nothing you dis-

-may, Re-member Christ our Sa-vi-our Was born on Christmas

Day, To save us all from Satan's pow'r When we were gone a-

CHORUS.
ff
-stray; O.. ti-dings of com-fort and joy, comfort and

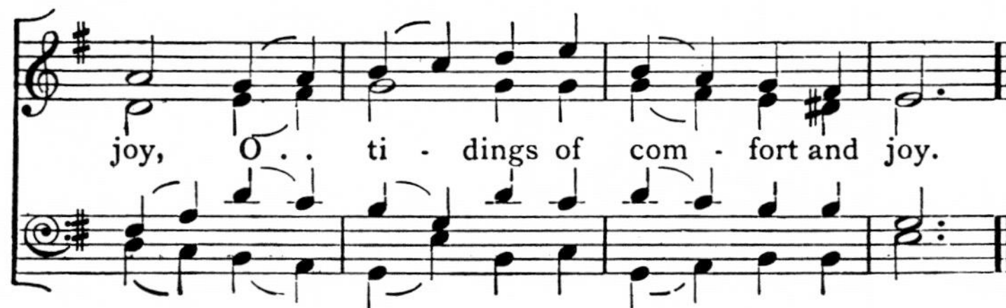
joy, O.. ti-dings of com-fort and joy.

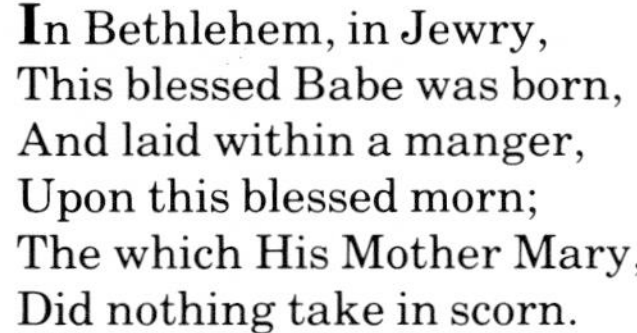

2

In Bethlehem, in Jewry,
This blessed Babe was born,
And laid within a manger,
Upon this blessed morn;
The which His Mother Mary,
Did nothing take in scorn.
O tidings, &c.

3

From God our Heavenly Father,
A blessed Angel came;
And unto certain Shepherds
Brought tidings of the same:
How that in Bethlehem was born
The Son of God by Name.
O tidings, &c.

4

"Fear not then," said the Angel,
"Let nothing you affright,
This day is born a Saviour
Of a pure Virgin bright,
To free all those who trust in Him
From Satan's power and might."
O tidings, &c.

5

The shepherds at those tidings
Rejoicèd much in mind,
And left their flocks a-feeding,
In tempest, storm, and wind:
And went to Bethlehem straightway,
The Son of God to find.
O tidings, &c.

— 6 —

And when they came to Bethlehem
Where our dear Saviour lay,
They found Him in a manger,
Where oxen feed on hay;
His Mother Mary kneeling down,
Unto the Lord did pray.
O tidings, &c.

— 7 —

Now to the Lord sing praises,
All you within this place,
And with true love and brotherhood
Each other now embrace;
This holy tide of Christmas
All other doth deface.
O tidings, &c.

A happy new Year to you!

A CRADLE-SONG OF THE BLESSED VIRGIN

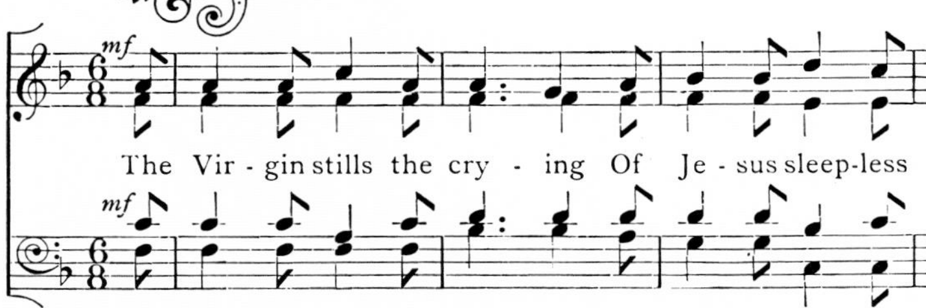
mf
The Vir - gin stills the cry - ing Of Je - sus sleep-less
mf

ly - ing; And sing - ing for His plea - sure Thus

più lento.
p
calls up - on her Trea - - sure, . My
p

Dar - ling, do not weep, My Je - su, sleep! . . .

— 2 —

O Lamb, my love inviting,
O Star, my soul delighting,
O Flower of mine own bearing,
O Jewel past comparing!
My Darling, &c.

— 3 —

My Child, of Might indwelling,
My Sweet, all sweets excelling,
Of Bliss the Fountain flowing,
The Dayspring ever glowing.
My Darling, &c

— 4 —

My Joy, my Exultation,
My spirit's Consolation;
My Son, my Spouse, my Brother,
O listen to Thy Mother.
My Darling, &c.

— 5 —

Say, wouldst Thou heavenly sweetness
Or love of answering meetness?
Or is fit music wanting?
Ho! Angels raise your chanting!
My Darling, &c.

TO GREET YOU

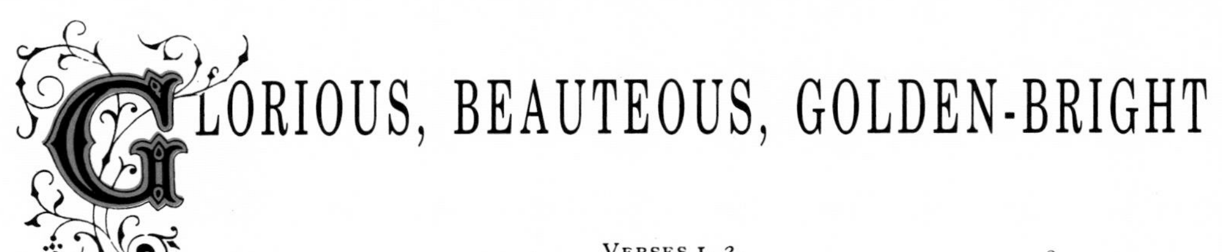

GLORIOUS, BEAUTEOUS, GOLDEN-BRIGHT

VERSES I, 2.

Glo - rious, beau-teous, gol - den - bright, Shed - ding

soft - est, pur - est light, Shone the stars that Christ-mas

night; When the Jew - ish shep - herds

kept Watch be - side their flocks that slept.

VERSES 3, 4, 5.

Soft and pure and ho - ly glory, Kings and seers and prophets

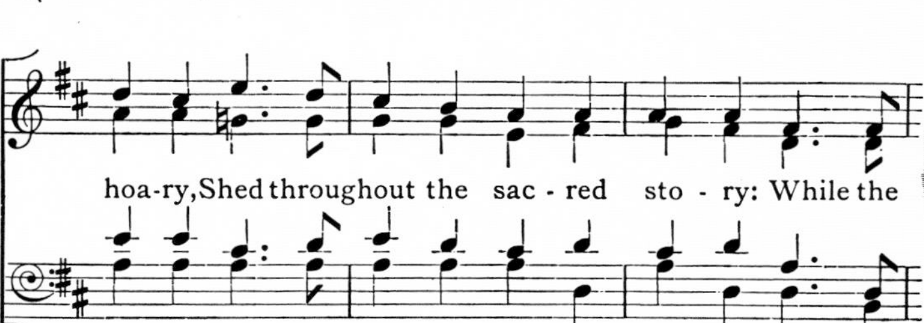
hoa-ry, Shed throughout the sac - red sto - ry: While the

— 2 —

But the stars' sweet golden gleam
Faded quickly as a dream
'Mid the wondrous glory-stream,
That illumined all the earth,
When Christ's angels sang His birth.

— 4 —

But that light no more availed,
All its splendour straightway paled
In His light whom angels hailed:
Even as the stars of old,
'Mid the brightness lost their gold.

— 5 —

Now no more on Christmas night,
Is the sky with angels bright,
But for ever shines the Light;
Even He whose birth they told
To the shepherds by the fold.

A JOYOUS
CHRISTMAS
AND
A HAPPY NEW YEAR.
D.L.R.
priests, like shepherds true, Watch'd beside God's cho-sen few.
mf VERSE 6.
Since that Light then dark - ens nev - er, Let us
all, with glad en - dea - vour, Sing the
rall. a tempo.
song that e-choes ev - er: Glo - ry in the high-est
pp rall.
Heav-en! Peace on earth to us for - giv - en.

MMANUEL, GOD WITH US

With spirit.
Joy fills our in - most heart to - day, The

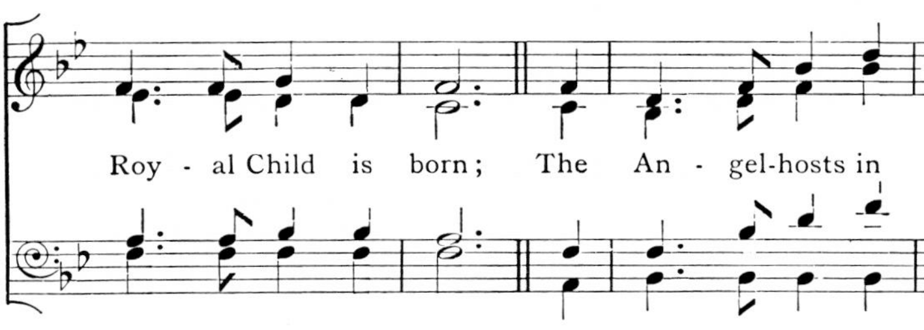
Roy - al Child is born; The An - gel-hosts in

glad ar - ray His ad - vent keep this morn.

In Unison.
The Ho - ly One is Ma - ry's Son, God

— 2 —

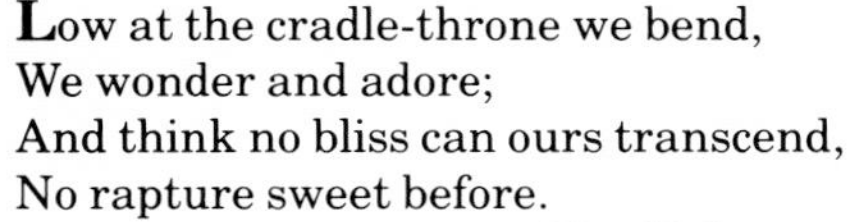

Low at the cradle-throne we bend,
We wonder and adore;
And think no bliss can ours transcend,
No rapture sweet before.
The Holy one, &c.

— 3 —

For us the world must lose its charms
Before the manger-shrine,
Where folded in Thy Mother's arms,
Thou sleepest, Babe Divine!
The Holy one, &c.

— 4 —

Angels are thronging round Thy bed,
Thine infant grace to see;
The stars are paling o'er Thy head,
The Day-spring dawns with Thee.
The Holy One, &c.

— 5 —

Thou art the very Light of Light,
Enlighten us, sweet Child,
That we may keep Thy Birthday bright,
With service undefiled.
The Holy One, &c.

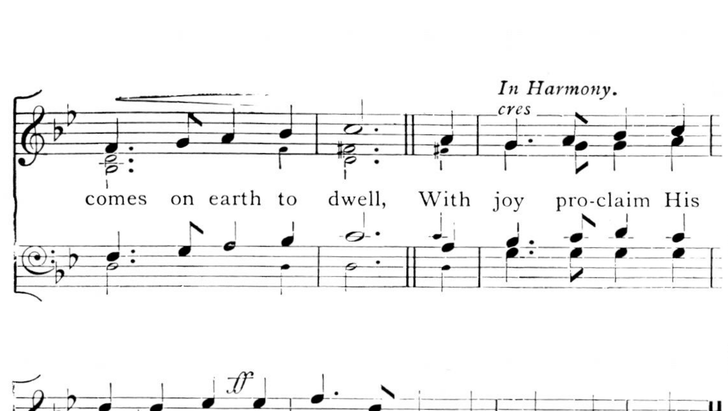
In Harmony.
cres
comes on earth to dwell, With joy pro-claim His
ff
glo-rious Name, Em - ma - nu - el, Em - ma - nu - el.

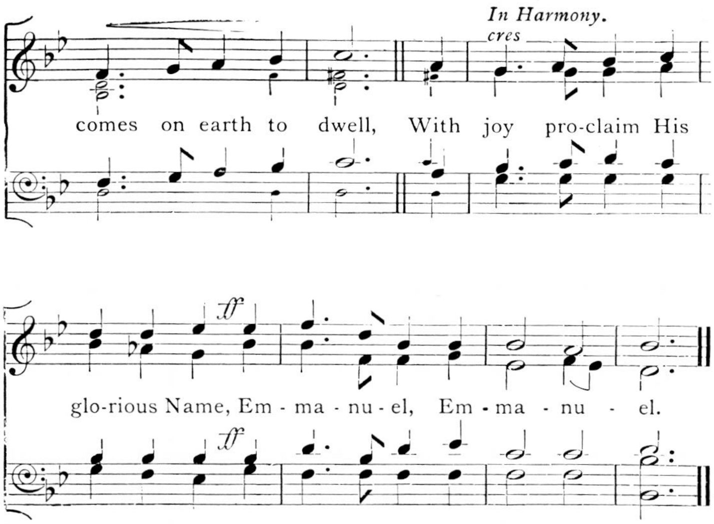

BRIGHT BE YOUR SEASON.
May you spend a joyous Christmas Day,
Full of fun and joy and merry play.

HE COVENTRY CAROL

p
Lul - lay, Thou lit - tle ti - ny Child,
p

cres.
mf
By, by, lul - ly, lul - lay: . . Lul - lay, Thou lit - tle
mf

dim.
pp rall.
ti - ny Child, By, by, lul - ly, lul - lay. . .
pp

— 2 —

O sisters too, how many we do,
For to preserve this day,
This poor Youngling for whom we sing
By, by, lully, lullay?

— 3 —

Herod the king in his raging,
Charged he hath this day
His men of might, in his own sight,
All children young to slay.

— 4 —

This woe is me, poor Child, for Thee,
And ever mourn and say,
For Thy parting nor say nor sing,
By, by, lully, lullay.

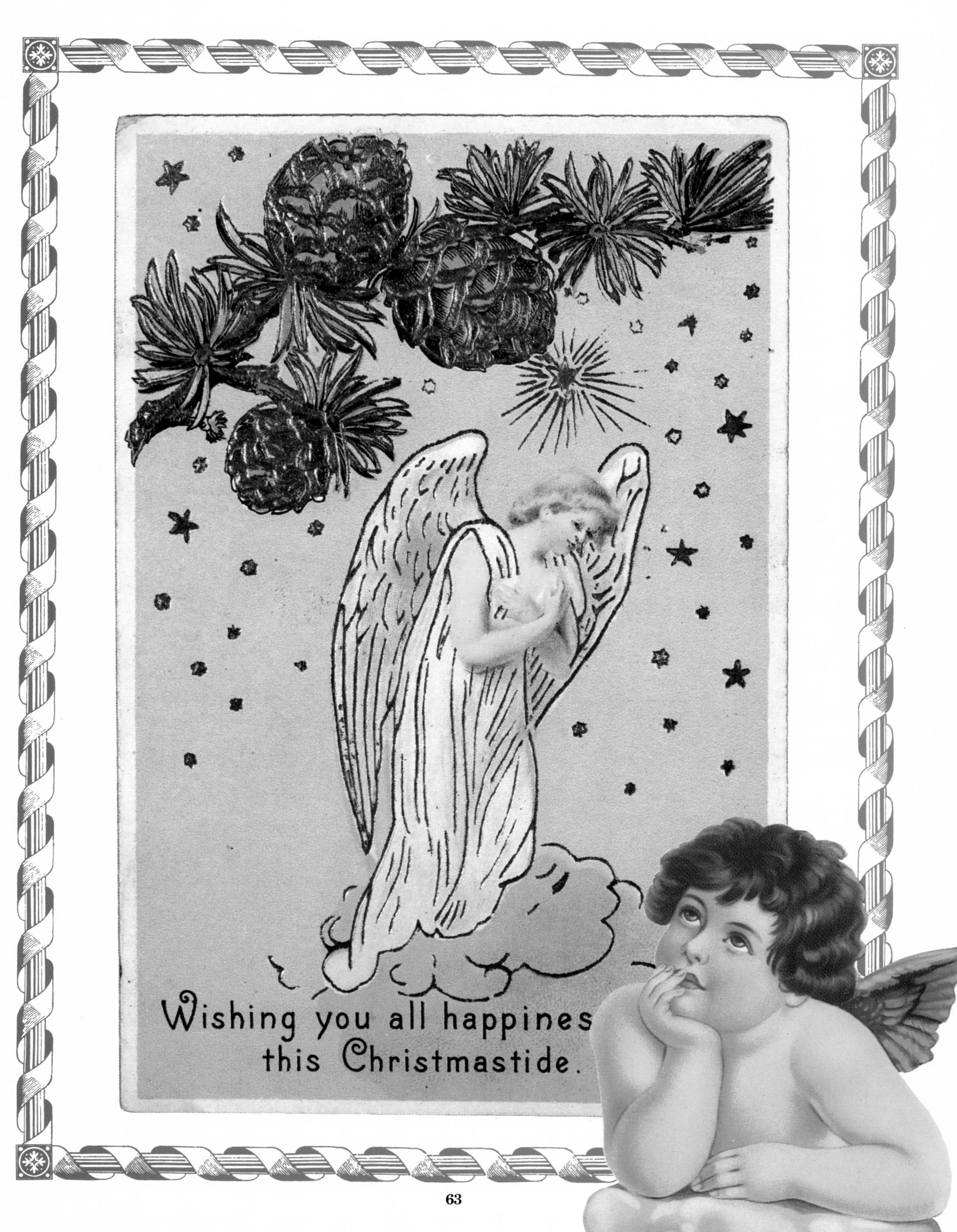
Wishing you all happines
this Christmastide.

OME, YE LOFTY

Come, Ye Lofty

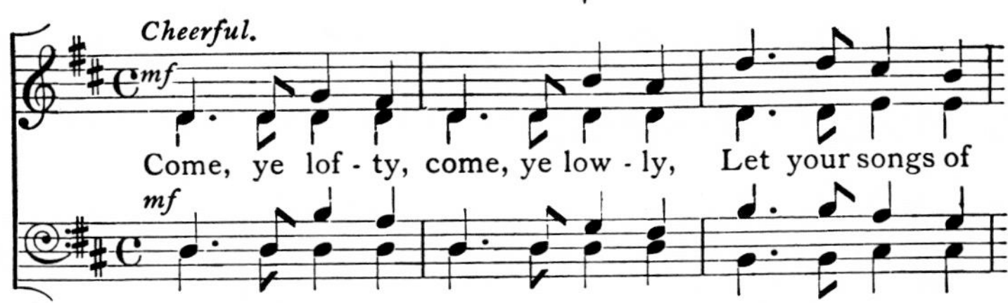
Cheerful.
mf
Come, ye lof - ty, come, ye low - ly, Let your songs of
mf

glad-ness ring; In a sta - ble lies the Ho - ly,

In a man - ger rests the King: See in Ma - ry's

arms re - pos - ing, Christ by high - est Heaven a - dored:

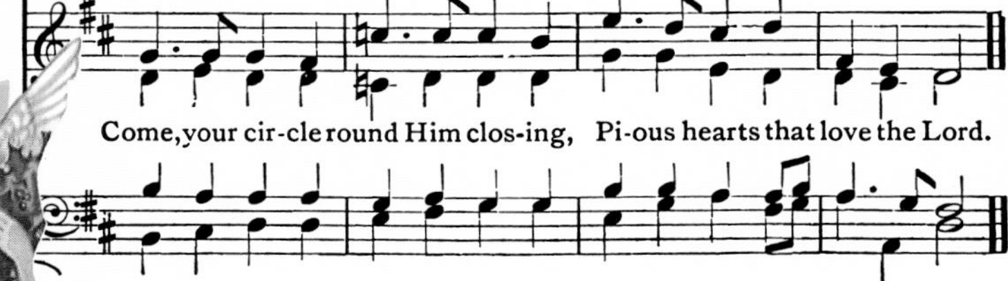
Come, your cir-cle round Him clos-ing, Pi-ous hearts that love the Lord.

— 2 —

Come, ye poor, no pomp of station
Robes the Child your hearts adore:
He, the Lord of all salvation,
Shares your want, is weak and poor:
Oxen, round about behold them;
Rafters naked, cold, and bare,
See the shepherds, God has told them
That the Prince of Life lies there.

— 3 —

Come, ye children, blithe and merry,
This one Child your model make;
Christmas holly, leaf, and berry,
All be prized for His dear sake;
Come, ye gentle hearts, and tender,
Come, ye spirits, keen and bold;
All in all your homage render,
Weak and mighty, young and old.

— 4 —

High above a star is shining,
And the Wisemen haste from far:
Come, glad hearts, and spirits pining:
For you all has risen the star.
Let us bring our poor oblations,
Thanks and love and faith and praise:
Come, ye people, come, ye nations.
All in all draw nigh to gaze.

— 5 —

Hark! the Heaven of heavens is ringing
"Christ the Lord to man is born!"
Are not all our hearts to singing,
"Welcome, welcome, Christmas morn?"
Still the Child, all power possessing,
Smiles as though the ages past;
And the song of Christmas blessing,
Sweetly sinks to rest at last.

I wish you
a Happy New Year.

JESU, HAIL! O GOD MOST HOLY

Je - su, hail! O God most ho - ly, Gen - tle Lamb, an
In - fant low - ly; Born, great God, a hu - man stran - ger,
Chorus.
Laid with - in the nar - row man - ger: Might tran - scend - ing
cres.
Weak - ness blend - ing, Greatness bend - ing from the sky;
Love un - end - ing, man be - friend - ing,
Last Verse.
God most High, God most High.

— 2 —

To enrich my desolation,
To redeem me from damnation,
Wrapt in swathing-bands Thou liest,
Thou in want and weakness sighest:
Might transcending, &c.

— 3 —

Low abased, where brutes are sleeping,
God's belovèd Son is weeping;
Judge supreme, true Godhead sharing,
Sinner's likeness for us wearing!
Might transcending, &c.

— 4 —

Jesu, Thine my heart is solely,
Draw it, take it to Thee wholly:
With Thy sacred Fire illume me,
Let it inwardly consume me.
Might transcending, &c.

— 5 —

Hence let idle fancies vanish,
Hence all evil passions banish;
Make me like Thyself in meekness,
Bind to Thee my human weakness.
Might transcending, &c.

THE FIRST NOWELL

mf
The first Now - ell the An - gel did
mf

say, Was to cer - tain poor shep-herds in fields as they

lay; In fields where they lay keep-ing their

sheep, On a cold win-ter's night that was so deep.

CHORUS.
ff
Now - ell, Now - ell, Now - ell, Now - ell, . .
ff

Born is the King of Is - - ra - el.

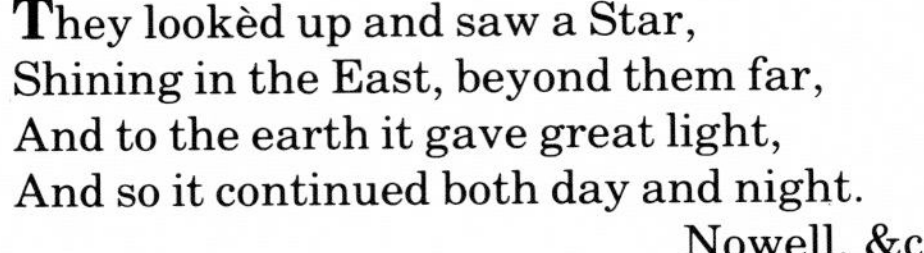

2

They lookèd up and saw a Star,
Shining in the East, beyond them far,
And to the earth it gave great light,
And so it continued both day and night.
Nowell, &c.

3

And by the light of that same Star,
Three Wisemen came from country far;
To seek for a King was their intent,
And to follow the Star wherever it went.
Nowell, &c.

4

This Star drew nigh to the north-west,
O'er Bethlehem it took its rest,
And there it did both stop and stay,
Right over the place where Jesus lay.
Nowell, &c.

5

Then entered in those Wisemen three,
Full reverently upon their knee,
And offered there, in His Presence,
Their gold, and myrrh, and frankincense.
Nowell, &c.

6

Then let us all with one accord,
Sing praises to our Heavenly Lord,
That hath made Heaven and earth of nought,
And with His Blood mankind hath bought.
Nowell, &c.

AKEN! CHRISTIAN CHILDREN

f
Wa-ken! Christ-ian child - ren, Up and let us sing,
f

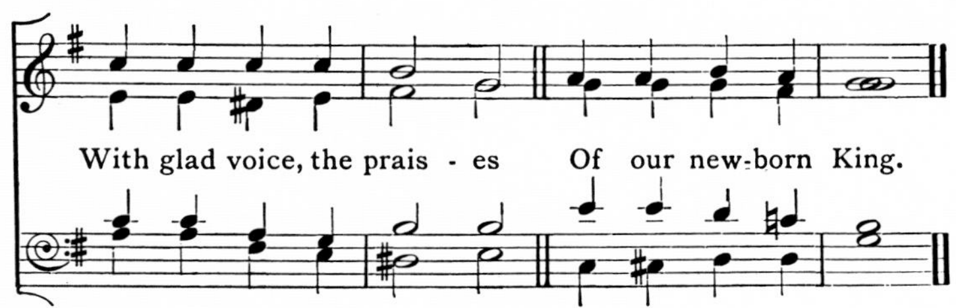
With glad voice, the prais - es Of our new-born King.

— 2 —

Up! 'tis meet to welcome,
With a joyous lay,
Christ, the King of Glory,
Born for us to-day.

— 3 —

Come, nor fear to seek Him,
Children though we be;
Once He said of chidren,
"Let them come to Me."

— 4 —

In a manger lowly,
Sleeps the heavenly Child;
O'er Him fondly bendeth
Mary, Mother mild.

— 5 —

Far above that stable,
Up in Heaven so high,
One bright star out-shineth,
Watching silently.

— 6 —

Fear not then to enter,
Though we cannot bring
Gold, or myrrh, or incense
Fitting for a King.

— 7 —

Gifts He asketh richer,
Offerings costlier still,
Yet may Christian children
Bring them if they will.

— 8 —

Brighter than all jewels
Shines the modest eye;
Best of gifts He loveth
Infant purity.

— 9 —

Haste we then to welcome,
With a joyous lay,
Christ, the King of Glory,
Born for us to-day.

Greetings

HAT SOUL-INSPIRING MUSIC

mf
What soul - in - spi-ring mu - sic Thrills thro' the midnight
mf

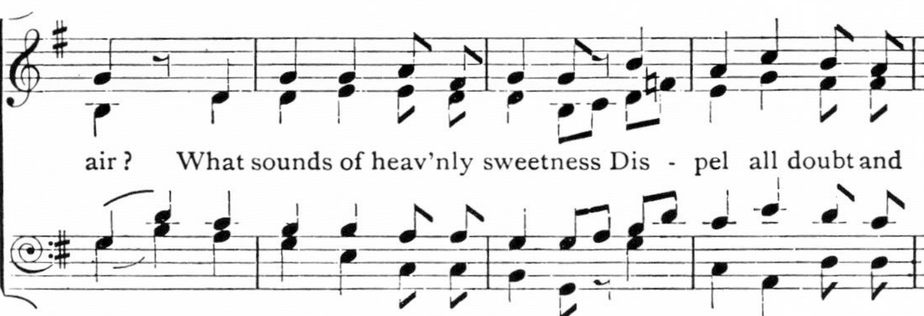
air ? What sounds of heav'nly sweetness Dis - pel all doubt and

f
care ? Ev' - ry star and con - stel - la - tion Sheds a
f

p
ra - diance dou - bly bright ; See the Plei - ads and O -
p

—— 2 ——

Strange forms float hovering o'er us,
New sounds fall on our ear;
God's Angel bids us welcome,
His voice says, "Never fear!
Born to you in David's city
Lies the Saviour, all Divine,
David's Root and David's Offspring,
Promised Seed of David's line:
He is swathed and in a manger;
Take this for a sign."

—— 3 ——

Straight, crowds of heavenly warriors,
Outshining every star,
Stand forth round that one Herald
Proclaiming peace afar;
Choirs of Angels and Archangels,
Seraphim and Cherubim,
Thrones and Princedoms, Dominations,
Powers and Might which wax not dim;
Spirit-hosts in ranks celestial,
Raise one joyous hymn.

DO

cres.
- ri - on Glit-ter keen - ly in the height! Spark-ling
f
fires, like twinkling blos-soms, Stud Night's robe with light.

— 4 —

"Lord God, to Thee be glory,
In heights all height above;
Peace dwell on earth beneath us,
Towards men goodwill and love!
Heaven and earth are now united,
Man may see his Father's face:
Mary's Son, God's Word incarnate,
Is an endless Fount of Grace:
Therefore Righteousness may Mercy
And Truth Peace embrace."

— 5 —

Speed, Shepherds, leave your sheepfolds,
To Bethle'm haste away:
Fall on your knees before Him,
Salute Him while ye may:
Bring your offerings, bring your treasure,
Open wide each simple store:
Pipe and dance in rustic measure
In his Manger Him adore:
Every deed to give Him pleasure
Be yours evermore.

OEL! NOEL!

mf
'Tis the day, the bles - sed day, On which our Lord was
mf

born, . . And sweet - ly do the sun - beams, gild The

dew - be-spang - led thorn. The birds sing through the

hea - vens clear, The breez - es gent - ly play, . . And

— 2 —

In an humble feeding-trough,
Within a lowly shed,
With cattle as His infant feet,
And shepherds at His head,
The Saviour of this sinful world
In innocence first lay,
And Wise-men made their offering
Upon an Holy day.
Noel, &c.

— 3 —

He will save the perishing,
Will waft the sighs to heaven
Of guilty men, who truly seek
And weep to be forgiven.
An intercessor still He shines,
And men to Him should pray,
Before His Altar meekly,
Upon this Holy Day.
Noel, &c.

— 4 —

Flowers, we see, bloom fair again,
Though all their life seems shed,
Thus we shall rise to life once more,
Though numbered with the dead,
Then may our station be near Him,
To whom we worship pay,
And offer hearty praises,
Upon this Holy day.
Noel, &c.

song and sun-shine love - ly Be - gin this Ho - ly Day. .
CHORUS.
No - el, No-el, No - el, No - el, No - el, No-el, No - el, . . Now
hear the sa - lu - ta - tion Of An - gel Ga - bri - el. . .
THE LORD CAME UPON THEM AND THE GLORY OF THE LORD SHONE
AND LO THE ANGEL OF
AND THE ANGEL SAID UN
TO THEM FEAR NOT FOR BEHOLD I BRING YOU GOOD TIDINGS OF GREAT

HAT CHILD IS THIS?

mf
What Child is this, who, laid to rest, On
mf

Ma - ry's lap is sleep - ing? Whom an-gels greet with

an - thems sweet, While shep-herds watch are keep - ing?

CHORUS.
ff
This, this is Christ the King; Whom
ff

— 2 —

Why lies He in such mean estate,
Where ox and ass are feeding?
Good Christian, fear: for sinners here
The silent Word is pleading:
Nails, spear, shall pierce Him through,
The Cross be borne, for me, for you:
Hail, hail, the Word made flesh,
The Babe, the Son of Mary!

— 3 —

So bring Him incense, gold and myrrh.
Come peasant, King to own Him;
The King of kings, salvation brings;
Let loving hearts enthrone Him.
Raise, raise, the song on high,
The Virgin sings her lullaby:
Joy, joy, for Christ is born,
The Babe, the Son of Mary!

shep-herds guard and an - gels sing: Haste, haste to

bring Him laud, The Babe, the Son of Ma - ry!

AND WHEN THEY WERE COME INTO THE HOUSE THEY SAW THE YOUNG CHILD WITH MARY HIS MOTHER AND FELL DOWN AND WORSHIPPED HIM ✱ AND WHEN THEY HAD OPENED THEIR TREASURES THEY PRESENTED UNTO HIM GIFTS GOLD AND FRANKINCENSE & MYRRH

Marcus Ward & Co.

ON THE BIRTHDAY OF THE LORD

Allegretto.
f
p
On the Birth-day of the Lord, An - gels joy in
f
p

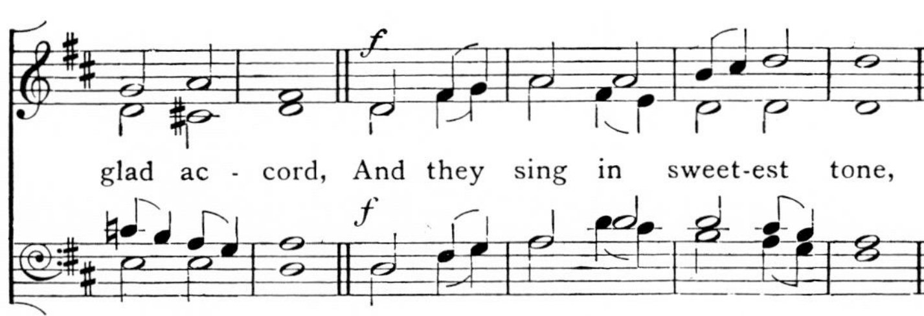
f
glad ac - cord, And they sing in sweet-est tone,
f

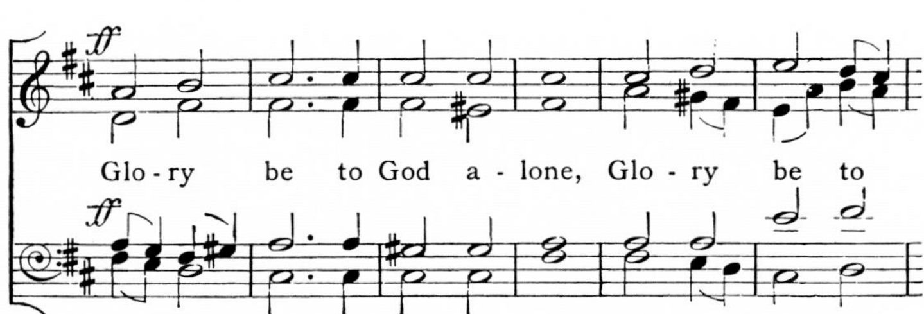
ff
Glo - ry be to God a - lone, Glo - ry be to
ff

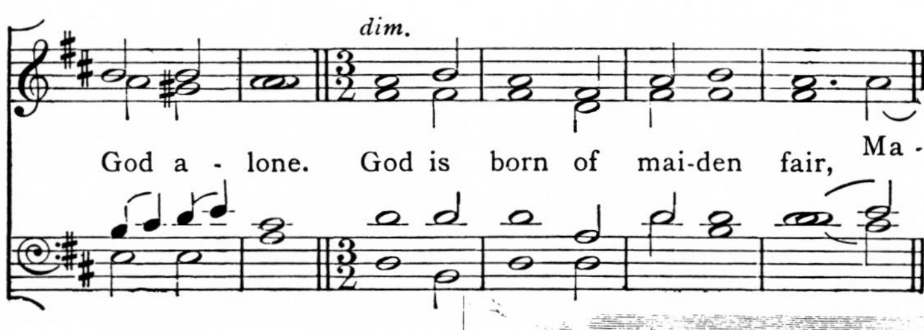
dim.
God a - lone. God is born of mai-den fair, Ma -

—— 2 ——

These good news an Angel told
To the shepherds by their fold,
Told them of the Saviour's Birth,
Told them of the joy for earth.
God is born, &c.

—— 3 ——

Born is now Emmanuel,
He, announced by Gabriel,
He, Whom Prophets old attest,
Cometh from His Father's Breast.
God is born, &c.

—— 4 ——

Born to-day is Christ the Child,
Born of Mary undefiled,
Born the King and Lord we own;
Glory be to God alone.
God is born, &c.

Ma - ry
cres.
dim.
- - - ry doth the Sa - viour bear; Ma - ry
Ma - ry
ev - er pure, . . . Ma - ry ev - er pure.
pp
pp

HE SEVEN JOYS OF MARY

mf
The first good joy that Ma - ry had, It was the joy of
mf

one; To see the bless - ed Je - sus Christ, When

Chorus.
ff
He was first her Son. When He was first her
ff

ff
Son, Good Lord; And hap - py may we be; . . Praise
ff

Fa-ther, Son, and Ho - ly Ghost To all e - ter - ni - ty.

— 2 —

The next good joy that Mary had,
It was the joy of two;
To see her own Son Jesus Christ
Making the lame to go.
Making the lame to go, Good Lord;
And happy, &c.

— 3 —

The next good joy that Mary had,
It was the joy of three;
To see her own Son Jesus Christ
Making the blind to see.
Making the blind to see, Good Lord;
And happy, &c.

— 4 —

The next good joy that Mary had,
It was the joy of four;
To see her own Son Jesus Christ
Reading the Bible o'er.
Reading the Bible o'er, Good Lord;
And happy, &c.

— 5 —

The next good joy that Mary had,
It was the joy of five;
To see her own Son Jesus Christ
Raising the dead to life.
Raising the dead to life, Good Lord;
And happy, &c.

— 6 —

The next good joy that Mary had,
It was the joy of six;
To see her own Son Jesus Christ
Upon the Crucifix.
Upon the Crucifix, Good Lord;
And happy, &c.

— 7 —

The next good joy that Mary had
It was the joy of seven;
To see her own Son Jesus Christ
Ascending into Heaven.
Ascending into Heaven, Good Lord;
And happy, &c.

SLEEP, HOLY BABE!

Sleep, Ho - ly Babe! up
on Thy mo-ther's breast; Great Lord of earth, and
sea, and sky, How sweet it is to see Thee lie

— 2 —

Sleep, holy Babe! Thine Angels watch around,
All bending low with folded wings,
Before the Incarnate King of kings,
In reverent awe profound.

— 3 —

Sleep, holy Babe! while I with Mary gaze
In joy upon that Face awhile,
Upon the loving infant smile
Which there divinely plays.

— 4 —

Sleep, holy Babe! ah! take Thy brief repose,
Too quickly will Thy slumbers break,
And Thou to lengthened pains awake,
That Death alone shall close.

dim.
pp
In such a place of rest. In such a place of
pp
rest. . . Accomp.

A VIRGIN UNSPOTTED

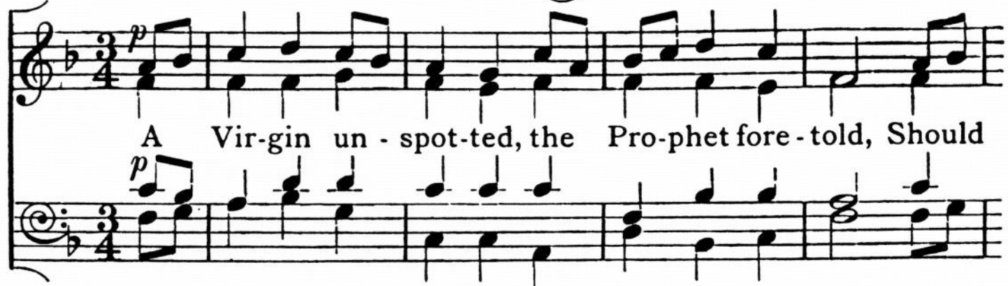
A Vir-gin un - spot-ted, the Pro-phet fore - told, Should

bring forth a Sav - iour, which now we be - hold,

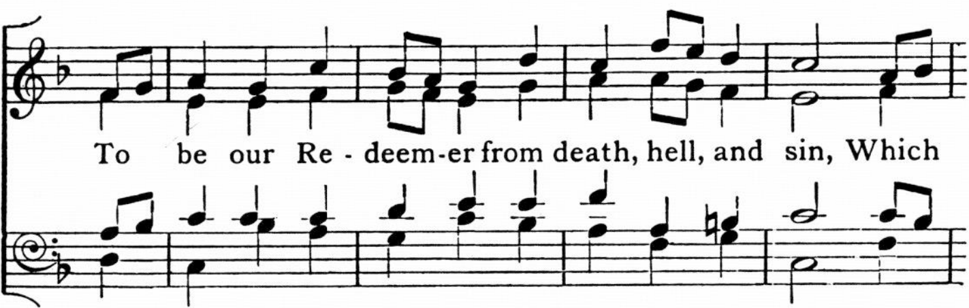
To be our Re - deem-er from death, hell, and sin, Which

— 2 —

At Bethlehem city in Jewry it was
That Joseph and Mary together did pass,
All for to be taxed with many one moe,
Great Caesar commanded the same should be so.
Aye and therefore, &c.

— 3 —

But when they had entered the city so fair,
A number of people so mighty was there,
That Joseph and Mary, whose substance was small,
Could find in the inn there no lodging at all.
Aye and therefore, &c.

— 4 —

Then were they constrained in a stable to lie,
Where horses and asses they used for to tie:
Their lodging so simple they took it no scorn,
But against the next morning our Saviour was born.
Aye and therefore, &c.

— 5 —

The King of all kings to this world being brought,
Small store of fine linen to wrap Him was sought;
But when she had swaddled her young Son so sweet;
Within an ox manger she laid Him to sleep.
Aye and therefore, &c.

A-dam's trans - gres - sion had wrap - ped us in.
CHORUS.
Aye and there-fore be mer - ry, set sor - row a -
side, Christ Je-sus our Sa-viour was born on this tide.
CHRISTMAS

— 6 —

Then God sent an angel from Heaven so high,
To certain poor shepherds in fields where they lie,
And bade them no longer in sorrow to stay,
Because that our Saviour was born on this day.
Aye and therefore, &c.

— 7 —

Then presently after the shepherds did spy
Vast numbers of angels to stand in the sky;
They joyfully talkèd and sweetly did sing,
To God be all glory, our heavenly King.
Aye and therefore, &c.

— 8 —

To teach us humility all this was done,
And learn we from thence haughty pride for to shun:
A manger His cradle who came from above,
The great God of mercy, of peace, and of love.
Aye and therefore, &c.

We Three Kings of Orient Are

mf
We three kings of O - rient are; Bear - ing gifts we tra - verse a - far Field and foun - tain, moor and mountain, Fol - low - ing yon - der star.
CHORUS. cres. ad lib. a tempo. ff
O Star of won - der, star of night, Star with roy - al beau - ty bright, West - ward lead - ing, still pro - ceed - ing, Guide us to Thy per - fect light.

— 2 —

Melchior.

Born a King on Bethlehem's plain,
Gold I bring, to crown Him again,
King for ever, ceasing never,
Over us all to reign.
O Star of wonder, &c

— 3 —

Caspar.

Frankincense to offer have I,
Incense owns a Deity nigh.
Prayer and praising, all men raising,
Worship Him, God most High.
O Star of wonder, &c.

— 4 —

Balthazar.

Myrrh is mine, its bitter perfume
Breathes a life of gathering gloom;
Sorrowing, sighing, bleeding, dying,
Sealed in the stone-cold tomb.
O Star of wonder, &c.

— 5 —

Glorious now behold Him arise,
King and God and sacrifice,
Alleluia, Alleluia;
Earth to the heavens replies.
O Star of wonder, &c.

When Christ Was Born of Mary Free

mf

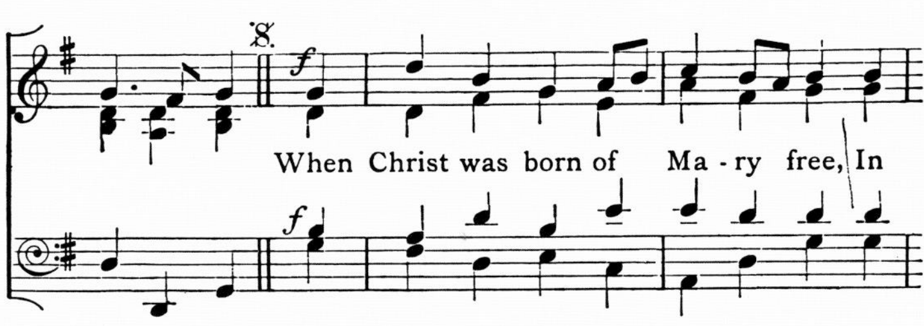
f
When Christ was born of Ma - ry free, In
f

Beth - le-hem that fair ci - tie, An - gels sang there with

p
mirth and glee, "In ex - cel - sis Glo - ri - a,
p

Chorus.
ff
In ex-cel-sis Glo-ri-a, In ex-cel-sis Glo-ri-a,
ff

— 2 —

Herdsmen beheld these Angels bright,
To them appearing with great light,
Who said God's Son is born to-night.
"In excelsis Gloria."

— 3 —

The King is come to save mankind,
As in Scripture truths we find,
Therefore this song we have in mind,
"In excelsis Gloria."

— 4 —

Then, dear Lord, for Thy great grace,
Grant us in bliss to see Thy face,
That we may sing to Thy solace,
"In excelsis Gloria."

In ex - cel - sis Glo - ri - a, In ex - cel - sis

D.S.
Glo - ri - a."

Verse 2.
Verse 4.
Herdsmen be-held, &c. Then, dear Lord, &c.

O THAT BLESSED GOING OUT

mf Allegro vivace.
ff
Wake all music's magic powers, On this blissful morn - ing,
mf
ff

mf
ff
Born to-day, the Child is ours, Theme of Prophet's warn-ing;
ff

mf
ff
Gi- ant in the race He towers, Toil and danger scorn - ing.
mf
ff

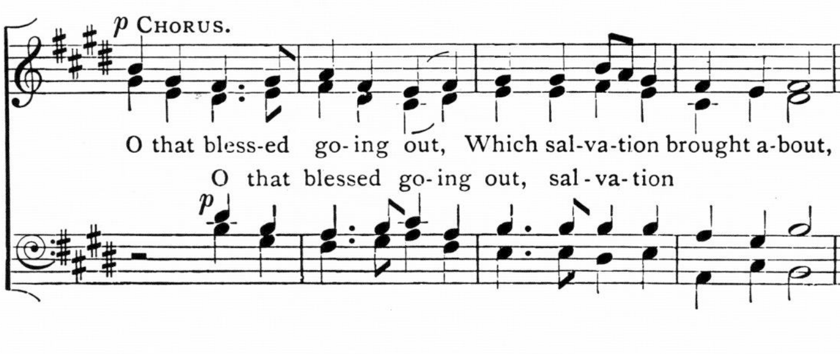
p Chorus.
O that bless-ed go- ing out, Which sal-va-tion brought a-bout,
O that blessed go- ing out, sal - va - tion
p

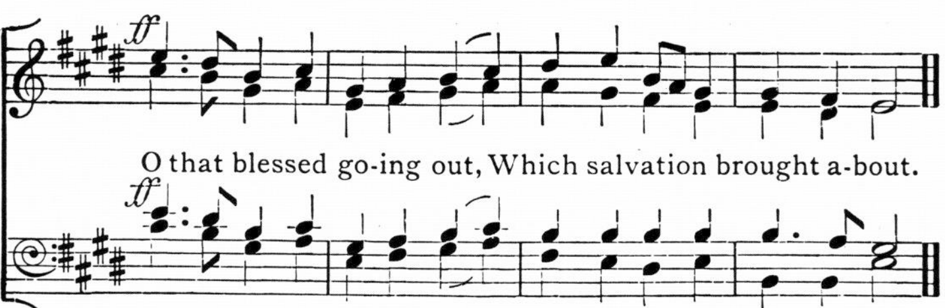
ff
O that blessed go-ing out, Which salvation brought a-bout.
ff

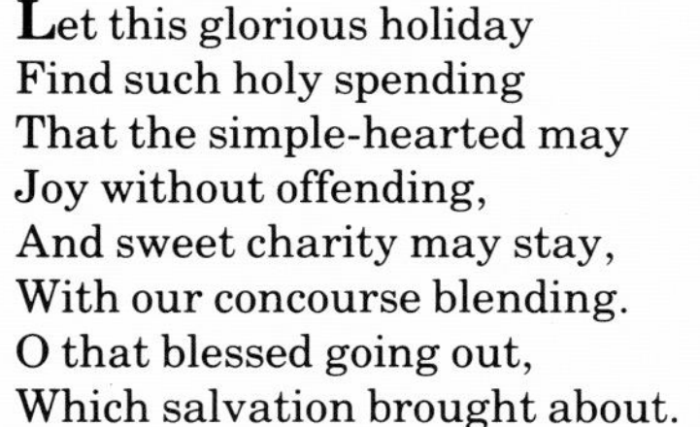

2

Let this glorious holiday
Find such holy spending
That the simple-hearted may
Joy without offending,
And sweet charity may stay,
With our concourse blending.
O that blessed going out,
Which salvation brought about.

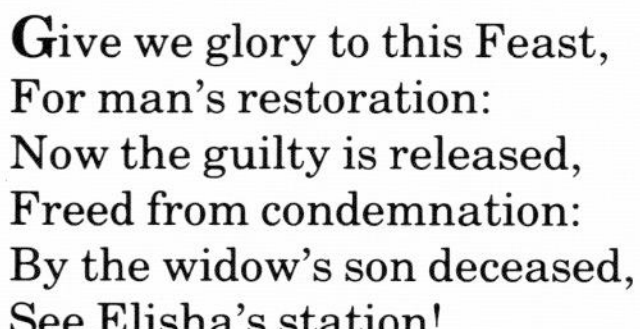

3

Give we glory to this Feast,
For man's restoration:
Now the guilty is released,
Freed from condemnation:
By the widow's son deceased,
See Elisha's station!
O that blessed, &c.

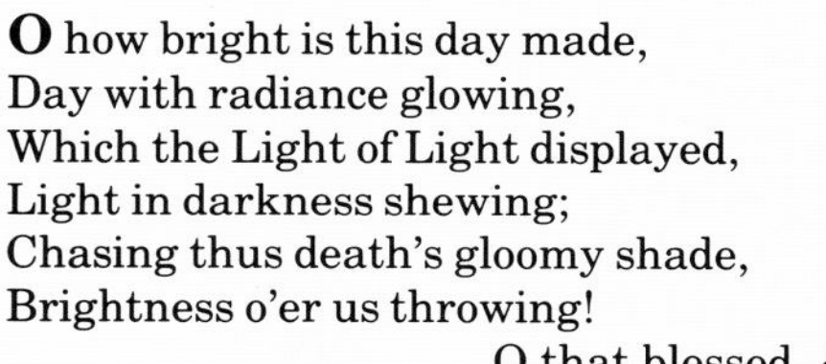

4

O how bright is this day made,
Day with radiance glowing,
Which the Light of Light displayed,
Light in darkness shewing;
Chasing thus death's gloomy shade,
Brightness o'er us throwing!
O that blessed, &c.

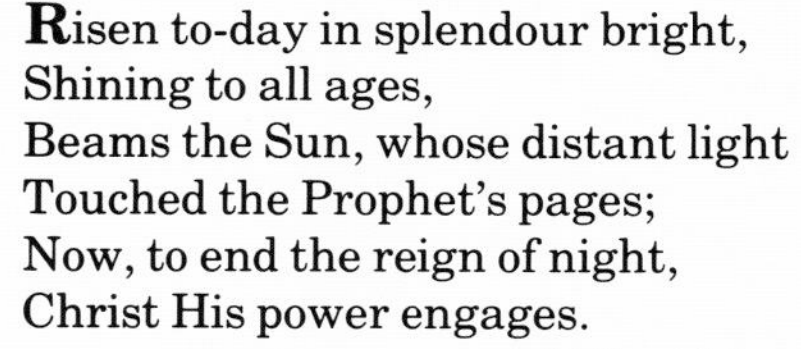

5

Risen to-day in splendour bright,
Shining to all ages,
Beams the Sun, whose distant light
Touched the Prophet's pages;
Now, to end the reign of night,
Christ His power engages.
O that blessed &c.

THE WASSAIL SONG

mf
Here we come a - was-sailing A-mong the leaves so
mf

green, Here we come a-wandering, So fair . . to be seen.

f CHORUS.
Love and joy come to you, And to you your was-sail
f

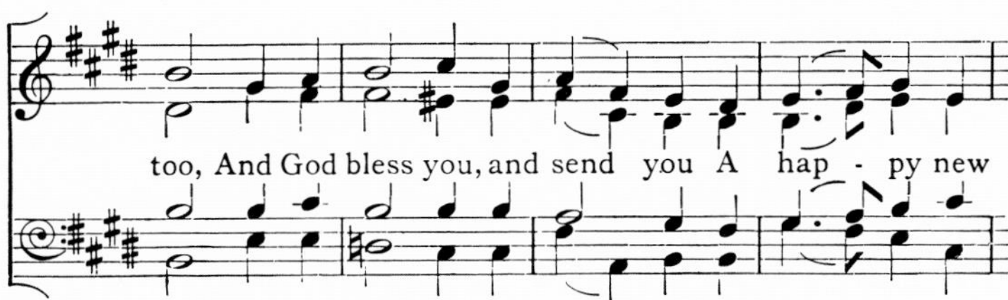
too, And God bless you, and send you A hap - py new

year, And God send you a hap-py new year.

* This note is required for verses 2, 3, 4, 5, 6 and 8.

— 2 —

Our wassail-cup is made
Of the rosemary tree,
And so is your beer
Of the best barley.
Love and joy, &c

— 3 —

We are not daily beggars
That beg from door to door,
But we are neighbours' children
Whom you have seen before.
Love and joy, &c

— 4 —

Good Master and good Mistress,
As you sit by the fire,
Pray think of us poor children
Who are wandering in the mire.
Love and joy, &c

— 5 —

We have a little purse
Made of ratching leather skin;
We want some of your small change
To line it well within.
Love and joy, &c

— 6 —

Call up the butler of this house,
Put on his golden ring;
Let him bring us a glass of beer,
And the better we shall sing.
Love and joy, &c

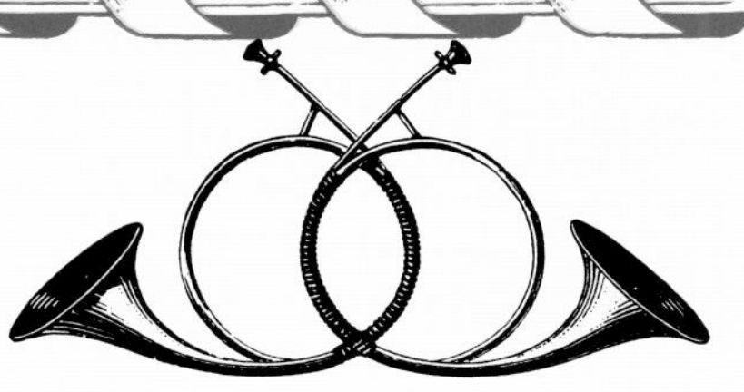

— 7 —

Bring us out a table,
And spread it with a cloth;
Bring us out a mouldy cheese,
And some of your Christmas loaf.
Love and joy, &c

— 8 —

God bless the master of this house,
Likewise the mistress too;
And all the little children
That round the table go.
Love and joy, &c

THE
WASSAIL
BOWL

OD'S DEAR SON

mf God's dear Son, with - out be - gin-ning, Whom the wick-ed
Jews did scorn; The on - ly wise, with-out all sin - ning,
On this bless-ed day was born: To save us all from
sin and thrall, When we in Sa-tan's chains were bound; And
shed His blood to do us good With many a pur-ple bleeding wound.

* This chord will be required for verses 3 and 4.
† This chord must be omitted in verses 2, 3, 5 and 6.

2

Bethlehem, King David's city,
Birth-place of that Babe we find,
God and Man, endued with pity,
And the Saviour of mankind:
Yet Jewry land, with cruel hand,
Both first and last His power denied;
When He was born they did Him scorn,
And shewed Him malice when He died.

3

No princely palace for our Saviour
In Judea could be found,
But sweet Mary's meek behaviour
Patiently upon the ground
Her Babe did place, in vile disgrace,
Where oxen in their stalls did feed;
No midwife mild had this sweet Child,
Nor woman's held at mother's need.

4

No kingly robes nor golden treasure
Decked the birth-day of God's Son;
No pompous train at all took pleasure
To the King of kings to run;
No mantle brave could Jesus have
Upon His cradle cold to lie;
No music's charms in nurse's arms
To sing that Babe a lullaby.

— 5 —

Yet, as Mary sat in solace
By our Saviour's cradle side,
Hosts of Angels from God's Palace,
Singing sweet through Heaven so wide;
Yea, Heaven and earth, at Jesu's Birth,
With sweet melodious tunes abound;
And every thing to Jewry's King.
Through all the world gives cheerful
sound.

— 6 —

Now to Him that hath redeemed us
By His Death on holy Rood,
And as sinners so esteemed us,
As to buy us with His Blood,
Yield lasting fame, that still the Name
Of Jesus may be honoured here;
And let us say that Christmas Day
Is still the best day in the year.

Joyeux
Noël!

WAS IN THE WINTER COLD

mf
'Twas in the win-ter cold, when earth Was de - so - late and
mf

f
dim.
p
wild, . . That an - gels welcomed at His birth The
f
p

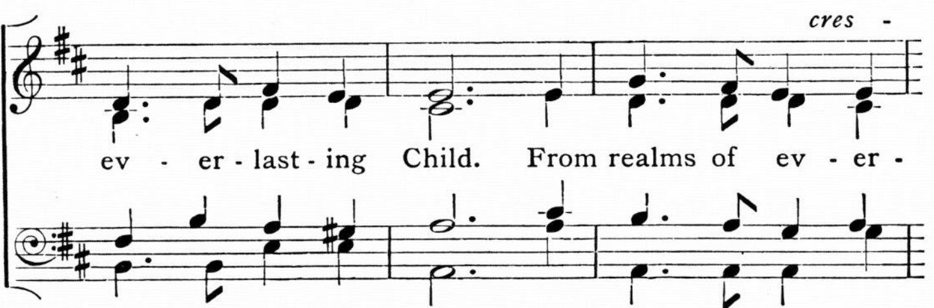
cres -
ev - er - last - ing Child. From realms of ev - er -

- cen - - - - do . . . poco . . .
- bright'ning day, And from His throne a - bove He

a . . . poco
f
p
rit. . . . . . .
came, with hu-man kind to stay, All low - li-ness and love.
f
p

—— 2 ——

Then in the manger the poor beast
Was present with his Lord;
Then swains and pilgrims from the East
Saw, wondered, and adored.
And I this morn would come with them
This blessed sight to see,
And to the Babe of Bethlehem
Bend low the reverent knee.

—— 3 ——

But I have not, it makes me sigh,
One offering in my power;
'Tis winter all with me, and I
Have neither fruit nor flower.
O God, O Brother, let me give
My worthless self to Thee;
And that the years which I may live
May pure and spotless be.

—— 4 ——

Grant me Thyself, O Saviour kind,
The Spirit undefiled,
That I may be in heart and mind
As gentle as a child;
That I may tread life's arduous ways
As Thou Thyself hast trod,
And in the might of prayer and praise
Keep ever close to God

—— 5 ——

Light of the everlasting morn,
Deep through my spirit shine;
There let Thy presence newly born
Make all my being Thine:
There try me as the silver, try,
And cleanse my soul with care,
Til Thou are able to descry
Thy faultless image there.

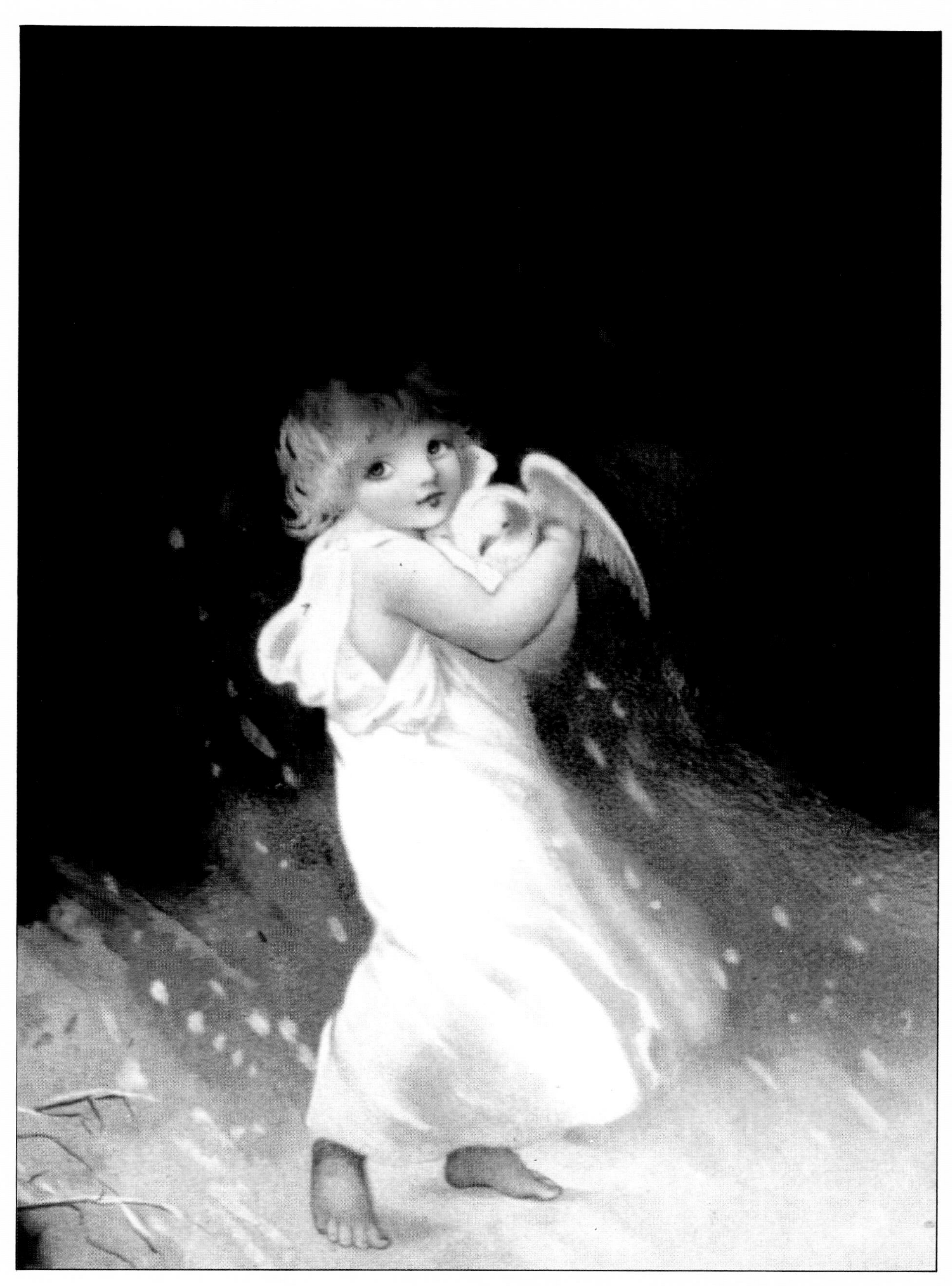

HE STORY OF THE SHEPHERD

p
It was the ve - ry noon of night: the stars a-bove the fold, More
p

mf
sure than clock or chim - ing bell, the hour of midnight told: When
mf

from the heavens there came a voice, and forms were seen to shine, Still

bright'ning as the mu - sic rose with light and love di - vine. With

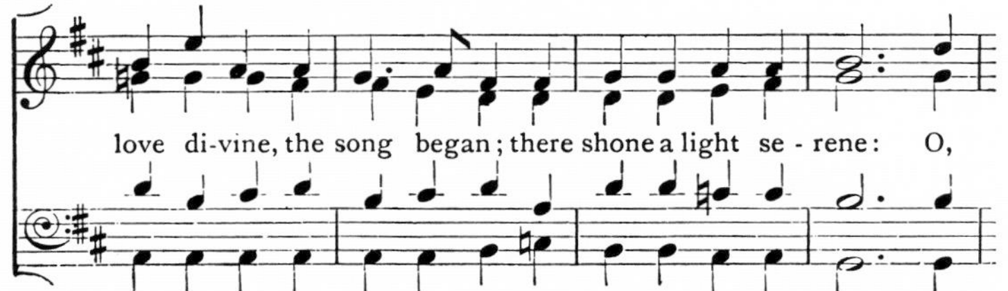

love di-vine, the song began; there shone a light se - rene: O,

— 2 —

O ne'er could nightingale at dawn salute
the rising day
With sweetness like that bird of song in
his immortal lay:
O ne'er were wood-notes heard at eve by
banks with poplar shade
So thrilling as the concert sweet by
heavenly harpings made;
For love divine was in each chord, and
filled each pause between:
O, who hath heard what I have heard, or
seen what I have seen?

— 3 —

I roused me at the piercing strain, but
shrunk as from the ray
Of summer lightning: all around so bright
the splendour lay.
For oh, it mastered sight and sense, to see
that glory shine,
To hear that minstrel in the clouds, who
sang of Love Divine,
To see that form with birdlike wings, of
more than mortal mien:
O, who hath heard what I have heard, or
seen what I have seen!

— 4 —

When once the rapturous trance was past,
that so my sense could bind,
I left my sheep to Him whose care
breathed in the western wind;
I left them, for instead of snow, I trod on
blade and flower,
And ice dissolved in starry rays at
morning's gracious hour,
Revealing where on earth the steps of
Love Divine had been;
O, who hath heard what I have heard, or
seen what I have seen?

who hath heard what I have heard, or seen what I have seen? O,
who hath heard what I have heard, or seen what I have seen?

— 5 —

I hasted to a low-roofed shed, for so the
Angel bade;
And bowed before the lowly rack where
Love Divine was laid:
A new-born Babe, like tender Lamb, with
Lion's strength there smiled,
For Lion's strength, immortal might, was
in that new-born Child;
That Love Divine in childlike form had
God for ever been:
O, who hath heard what I have heard, or
seen what I have seen?

BABE IS BORN

mf
A Babe is born, all of a Maid, To
mf

bring sal - va - tion un - to us; No more are we to

sing a - fraid, Ve - ni, Cre - a - tor Spi - ri - tus.

2

At Bethlehem, that blessed place,
The Child of bliss then born He was;
Him aye to serve God give us grace,
O Lux beata Trinitas.

3

There came three kings out of the East,
To worship there that King so free;
With gold and myrrh and frankincense,
A solis ortus cardine.

4

The shepherds heard an Angel cry,
A merry song that night sang he,
Why are ye all so sore aghast,
Fam lucis orto sidere?

5

The Angel came down with a cry,
A fair and joyful song sang he,
All in the worship of that Child,
Gloria Tibi Domine.

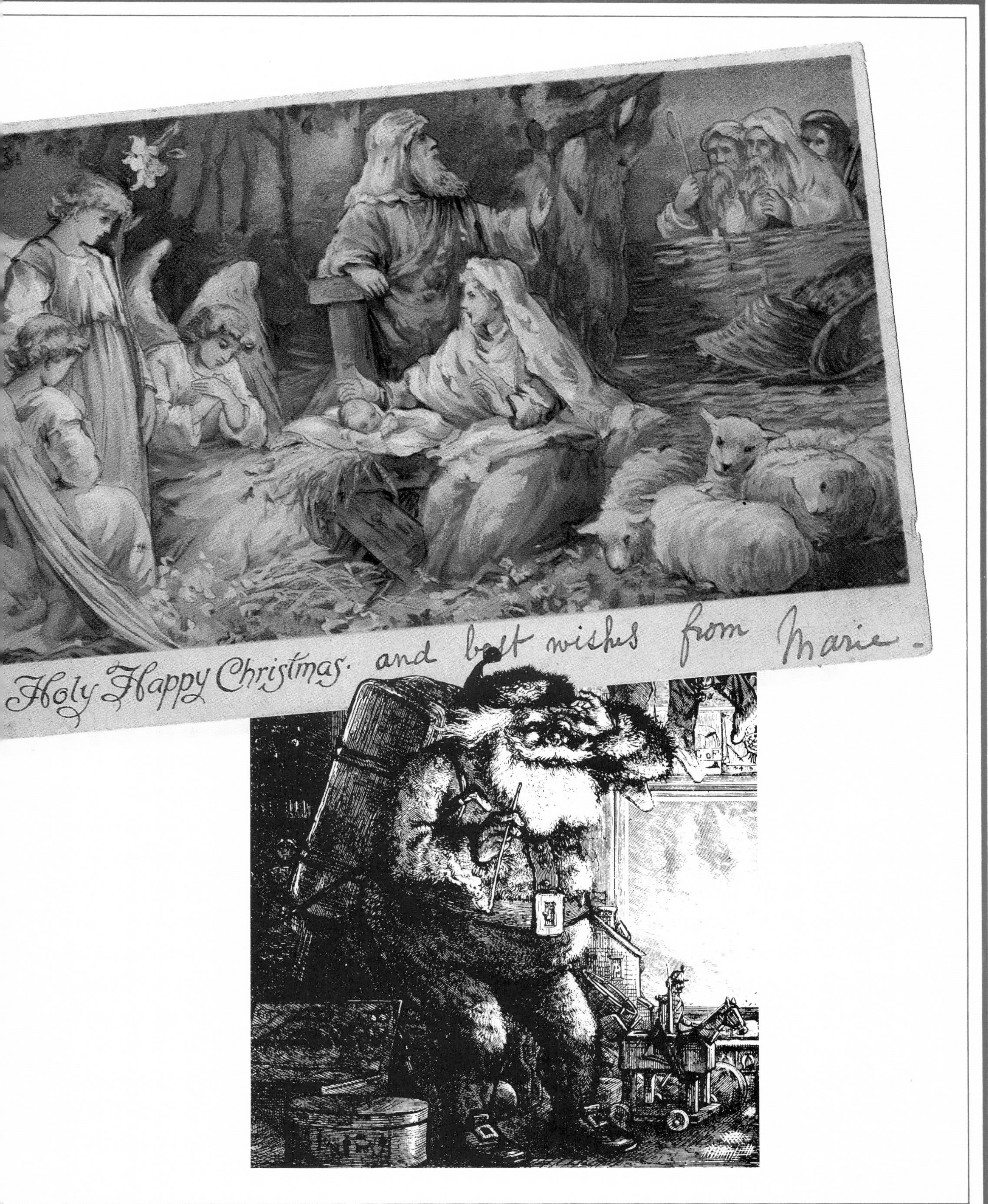
Holy Happy Christmas. and best wishes from Marie.

THE BOY'S DREAM

Andante.
Last night as I was laid and slept, When all my prayers were

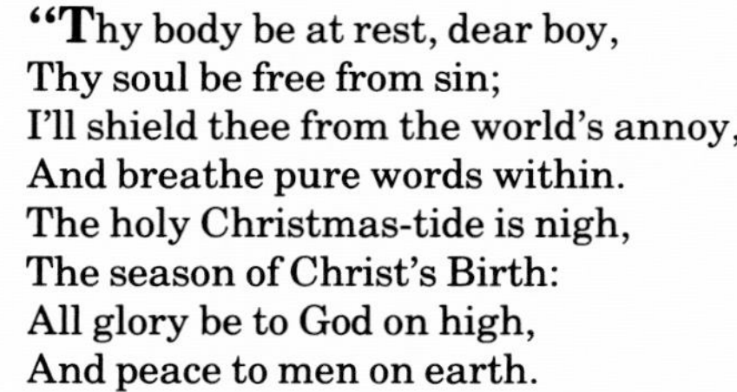

— 2 —

"Thy body be at rest, dear boy,
Thy soul be free from sin;
I'll shield thee from the world's annoy,
And breathe pure words within.
The holy Christmas-tide is nigh,
The season of Christ's Birth:
All glory be to God on high,
And peace to men on earth.

said; While still my guard-ian An - gel kept His

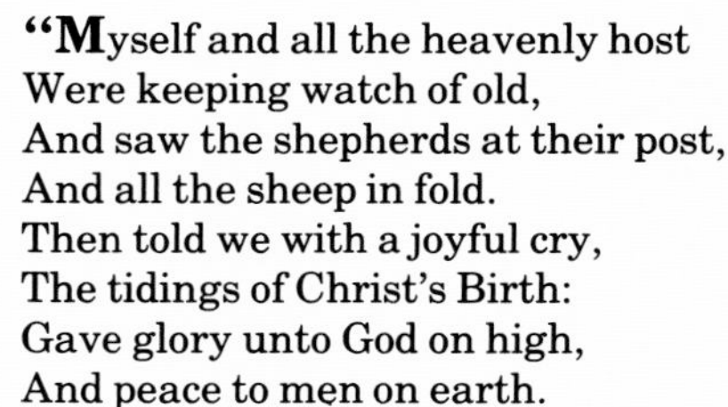

— 3 —

"Myself and all the heavenly host
Were keeping watch of old,
And saw the shepherds at their post,
And all the sheep in fold.
Then told we with a joyful cry,
The tidings of Christ's Birth:
Gave glory unto God on high,
And peace to men on earth.

watch a - bove my head; I heard his sweet voice

— 4 —

"He bowed to all His Father's will,
And meek was He and lowly;
And year by year His thoughts were still
Most innocent and holy.
He did not come to strive or cry,
But ever from His Birth
Gave glory unto God on high,
And peace to men on earth."

car - ol - ling, Full soft - ly in my ear, A

— 5 —

"Like Him be true, like Him be pure,
Like Him be full of love;
Seek not thine own, and so secure
Thine own which is above:
And still when Christmas-tide
draws nigh,
Sing thou of Jesus' Birth;
All glory be to God on high,
And peace to men on earth."

song for Christian boys to sing, For Christian men to hear.

GLAD
BE THY
CHRISTMAS.

THE SHEPHERDS AMAZED

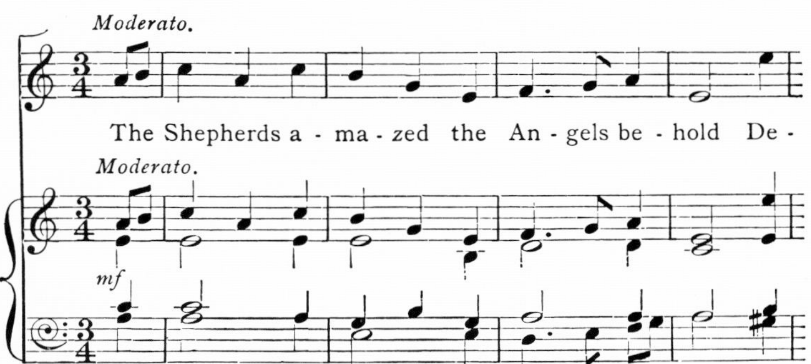
Moderato.
The Shepherds a - ma - zed the An - gels be - hold De -
Moderato.
mf

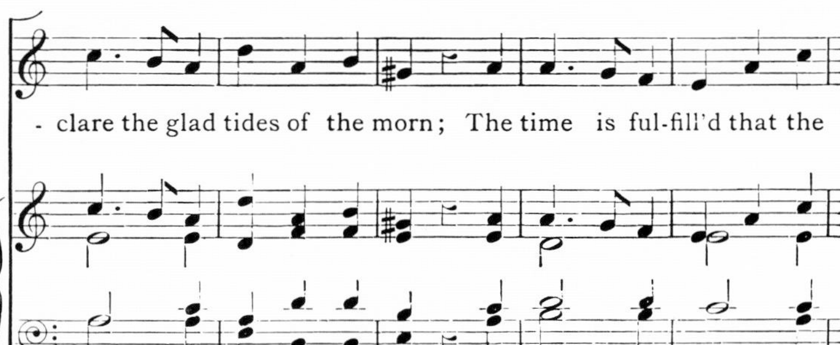
- clare the glad tides of the morn; The time is ful-fill'd that the

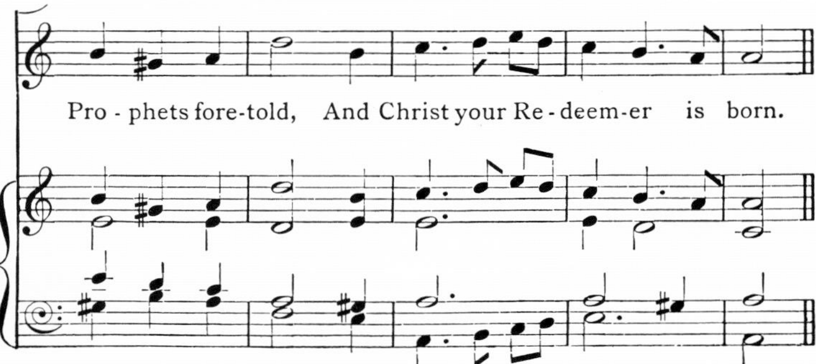
Pro - phets fore-told, And Christ your Re - deem-er is born.

2

Behold, in a manger the Lord He is laid,
Who came our salvation to bring;
Go seek Him, ye shepherds, and be not afraid,
He is your Redeemer and King.
All glory and honour, &c.

3

In Bethlehem city the Prophets agree
A Virgin should bring forth a Son;
Go haste to the stable, ye shepherds, and see,
For as it was said it is done.
All glory and honour, &c.

4

The shepherds obeyed, and the Babe did espy,
The Angels most sweetly did sing;
Let's join in their songs to the great God on high,
For sending our Saviour and King.
All glory and honour, &c.

Chorus.
All glo - ry and ho - nour to God our Cre - a - tor, Who
came from His glo - ry on high; In hum - ble sub - mis - sion took
on Him our na - ture, That we might par - take of His joy.

AWAY IN A MANGER

Lightly, moderately quickly
A - way in a manger, no crib for a bed, The little Lord Je - sus laid down His sweet head; The stars in the bright sky looked down where He lay, The little Lord Je - sus a - sleep on the hay.
Verses 1 and 2
Verse 3
live with Thee there.

—— 2 ——

The cattle are lowing, the baby awakes;
But little Lord Jesus, no crying He makes:
I love Thee, Lord Jesus; look down from the sky,
And stay by my side until morning is nigh.

—— 3 ——

Be near me, Lord Jesus; I ask Thee to stay
Close by me for ever, and love me, I pray;
Bless all the dear children in Thy tender care,
And fit us for heaven to live with Thee there.

COME, TUNE YOUR HEART

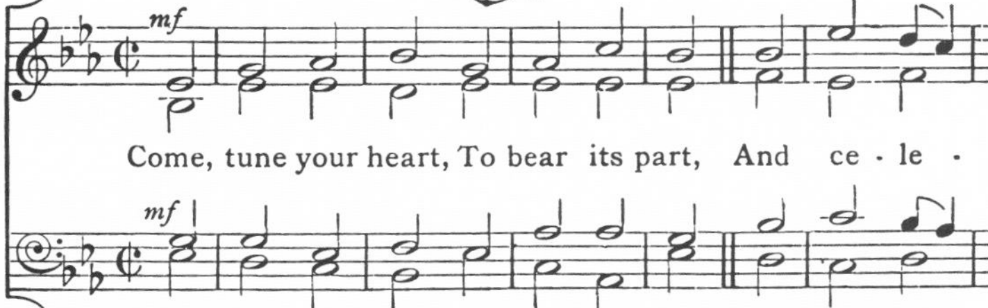
mf
Come, tune your heart, To bear its part, And ce - le -
mf

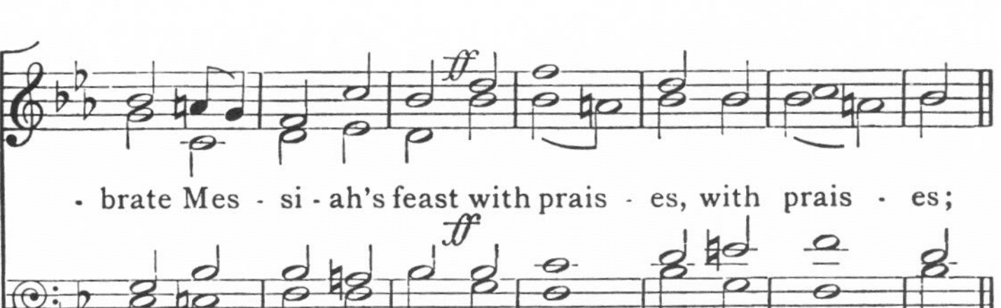
ff
- brate Mes - si - ah's feast with prais - es, with prais - es;
ff

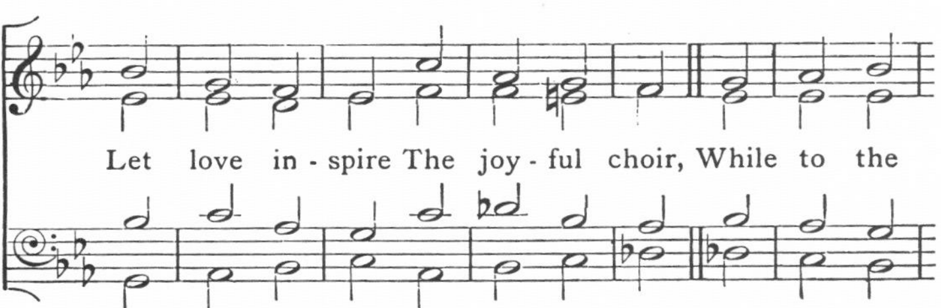
Let love in - spire The joy - ful choir, While to the

God of Love glad hymns it rais - es, it rais - es.

— 2 —

Exalt His Name;
With joy proclaim,
God loved the world, and through His Son forgave us;
Oh! what are we,
That, Lord, we see
Thy wondrous love, in Christ who died to save us!

— 3 —

Your refuge place
In His free grace,
Trust in His Name, and day by day repent you;
Ye mock God's Word,
Who call Him Lord,
And follow not the pattern He hath lent you.

— 4 —

O Christ, to prove
For Thee my love,
In brethren Thee my hands shall clothe and cherish;
To each sad heart
Sweet Hope impart,
When worn with care, with sorrow nigh to perish.

— 5 —

Come, praise the Lord;
In Heaven are stored
Rich gifts for those who here His Name esteemèd;
Alleluia,
Alleluia;
Rejoice in Christ, and praise Him, ye redeemèd.

THE MANGER THRONE

For Verses 1, 4, 5.
mf
Like sil - ver lamps in a dis - tant shrine, The
mf

stars are spark -ling bright; The bells of the ci - ty of

God ring out, For the Son of Ma-ry was born to-night; The

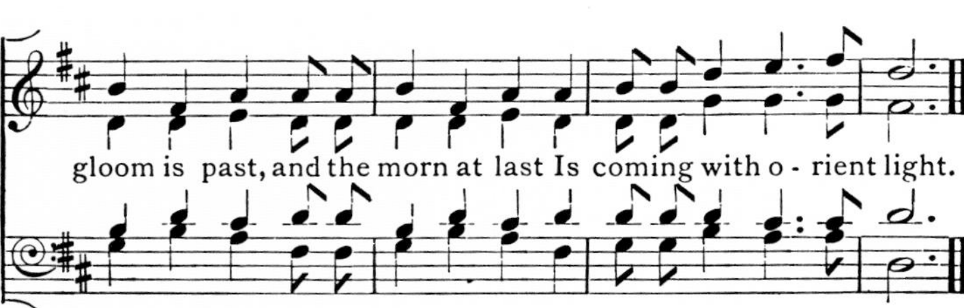
gloom is past, and the morn at last Is coming with o - rient light.

For Verses 2, 3.
2. Ne-ver fell me-lo-dies half so sweet As those which are filling the

— 3 —

Now a new Power has come on the earth,
A match for the armies of Hell:
A Child is born who shall conquer the foe,
And all the spirits of wickedness quell;
For Mary's Son is the Mighty One
Whom the prophets of God foretell.

— 4 —

The stars of heaven still shine as at first
They gleamed on this wonderful night;
The bells of the city of God peal out,
And the Angels' song still rings in the height;
And love still turns where the Godhead burns,
Hid in Flesh from fleshly sight.

— 5 —

Faith sees no longer the stable-floor,
The pavement of sapphire is there,
The clear light of Heaven streams out to the world:
And Angels of God are crowding the air;
And Heaven and earth, through the spotless Birth,
Are at peace on this night so fair.

skies; And nev-er a pa-lace shone half so fair As the
man-ger bed where our Sa-viour lies; No night in the year is
half so dear As this which has end-ed our sighs.

THE MOON SHINES BRIGHT

Moderato.
mf 1. The moon shines bright and the stars give a light A
little be - fore the day, Our migh - ty Lord He
looked on us, And bade us a-wake and pray.

— 2 —

Awake, awake, good people all,
Awake,and you shall hear,
The Lord our God died on the Cross,
For us He loved so dear.

— 3 —

O fair, O fair Jerusalem,
When shall I come to thee?
When shall my sorrows have an end,
The joy that I may see?

— 4 —

The fields were green as green could be,
When from His glorious seat
Our blessed Father watered us
With His heavenly dew so sweet.

— 5 —

And for the saving of our souls
Christ died upon the cross,
We ne'er shall do for Jesus Christ,
As He hath done for us.

A merry Christmas

— 6 —

The life of man is but a span,
And cut down in its flower,
We're here to-day, to-morrow gone,
The creatures of an hour.

— 7 —

Instruct and teach your children well,
The while that you are here;
It will be better for your soul,
When your corpse lies on the bier.

— 8 —

To-day you may be alive and well,
Worth many a thousand pound;
To-morrow dead and cold as clay,
Your corpse laid underground.

— 9 —

With one turf at thine head,
  O man,
And another at Thy feet;
Thy good deeds and thy bad,
  O man,
Will all together meet.

— 10 —

My song is done, I must be gone,
I can stay no longer here;
God bless you all, both great and small,
And send you a joyful new year!

WHEN THE CRIMSON SUN HAS SET

When the crimson sun had set Low behind the wintry sea,
On the bright And cold midnight Burst a sound of heavenly glee:

Glo - - - - - - ri - a in ex-cel-sis De - o,

Glo - - - - - - - ri - a in ex-cel-sis De - - o.

p
pp
cres.
rall. e dim.
sing, The world in sol-emn si-lence lay To hear the Angels sing.

— 2 —

Shepherds watching by their fold,
On the crisp and hoary plain,
In the sky
Bright Hosts espy,
Singing in a gladsome strain, Gloria, &c.

— 3 —

Where the manger crib is laid,
In the city fair and free,
Hand in hand
This Shepherd band
Worship CHRIST on bended knee.
Gloria, &c.

— 4 —

Join with us in welcome song,
Ye who in Christ's Home abide,
Sing the Love
Of God above,
Shown at happy Christmas-tide.
Gloria, &c.

ONCE IN ROYAL DAVID'S CITY

Once in royal Da - vid's ci - ty Stood a lowly cat - tle shed,

Where a Mother laid her Ba - by In a manger for His bed;

Mary was that Mother mild, JESUS CHRIST her on - ly CHILD.

—— 2 ——

He came down to earth from Heaven,
Who is God and Lord of all,
And His shelter was a stable,
And His cradle was a stall;
With the poor, and mean, and lowly,
Lived on earth our Saviour holy.

—— 3 ——

And through all His wondrous Childhood,
He would honour and obey,
Love and watch the lowly Maiden,
In whose gentle arms He lay;
Christian children all must be
Mild, obedient, good, as He.

—— 4 ——

For He is our childhood's pattern,
Day by day like us He grew,
He was little, weak, and helpless,
Fears and smiles like us He knew,
And He feeleth for our sadness,
And He shareth in our gladness.

—— 5 ——

And our eyes at last shall see Him,
Through His own redeeming love,
For that Child, so dear and gentle,
Is our Lord In Heaven above;
And He leads His children on
To the place where He is gone.

—— 6 ——

Not in that poor lowly stable,
With the oxen standing by,
We shall see Him; but in Heaven,
Set at God's right Hand on High;
When like stars His children crowned,
All in white, shall wait around.

Christmas Joys
be thine.

T CAME UPON THE MIDNIGHT CLEAR

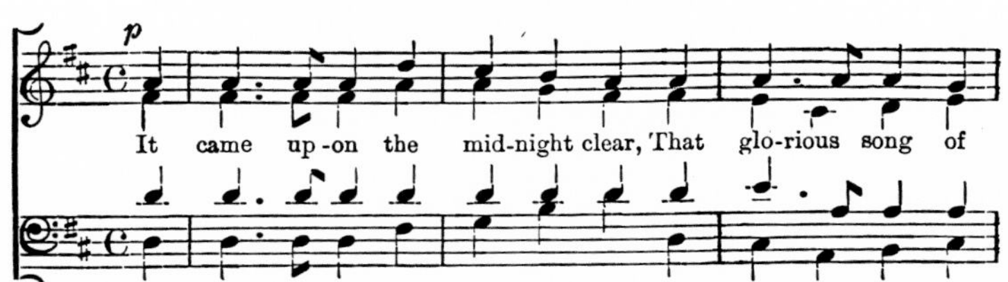

p
It came up-on the mid-night clear, That glo-rious song of

p
cres.
old, From An - gels bend- ing near the earth With news of joy fore-

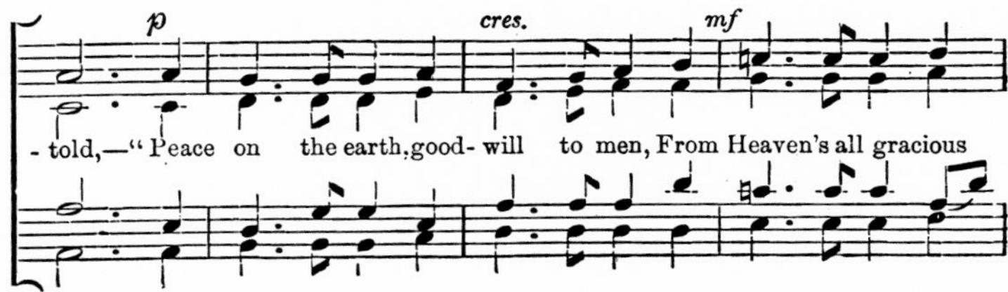

p
cres.
mf
- told,—" Peace on the earth, good- will to men, From Heaven's all gracious

p
pp
cres.
KING." The world in sol -emn si - lence lay To hear the An - gels

p
pp
cres.
rall. e dim.
sing, The world in sol-emn si-lence lay To hear the Angels sing.

—— 2 ——

Still through the cloven skies they come,
Love's banner all unfurled;
And gladsome, too, their music floats
O'er all the busy world:
Above its sad and lowly plains
Old echoes plaintive ring,
For ever o'er its Babel sounds
The blessed Angels sing.

—— 3 ——

Yet with the woes of sin and strife
The world has suffered long;
Beneath the Angel-strain have rolled
Two thousand years of wrong;
And man at war with man hears not
The love-song which they bring;
Oh! hush the noise, ye men of strife,
And hear the Angels sing.

—— 4 ——

For lo, the days are hastening on,
By prophet-bards foretold,
When with the ever-circling years,
Comes round the age of gold,
When peace shall over all the Earth
Its ancient splendours fling,
And the whole world send back the song
Which now the Angels sing.

HE CHERRY TREE CAROL

mf *
Jo - seph was an old man, An
mf

old man was he: He mar - ried sweet

Ma - ry, The Queen of Ga - li - lee.

— 8 —

As Joseph was a-walking
He heard Angels sing,
"This night there shall be bor
Our heavenly King.

— 9 —

"**H**e neither shall be born
In house nor in hall,
Nor in the place of Paradise,
But in an ox-stall.

— 10 —

"**H**e shall not be clothēd
In purple nor pall;
But all in fair linen,
As wear babies all.

— 11 —

"**H**e shall not be rocked,
In silver nor gold,
But in a wooden cradle
That rocks on the mould.

— 2 —

As they went a walking
In the garden so gay,
Maid Mary spied cherries
Hanging over yon tree.

— 3 —

Mary said to Joseph,
With her sweet lips so mild,
"Pluck those cherries, Joseph,
For to give to my Child."

— 3 —

"**O** then," replied Joseph,
With words so unkind,
"I will pluck no cherries
For to give to thy Child."

— 4 —

Mary said to cherry tree,
"Bow down to my knee,
That I may pluck cherries
By one, two, and three."

— 6 —

The uppermost sprig then
Bowed down to her knee:
"Thus you may see, Joseph,
These cherries are for me."

— 7 —

"**O** eat your cherries, Mary,
O eat your cherries now,
O eat your cherries, Mary,
That grew upon the bough."

— 12 —

"**H**e neither shall be christened
In milk nor in wine,
But in pure spring well water
Fresh sprung from Bethine."

— 13 —

Mary took her Baby
She dressed Him so sweet,
She laid Him in a manger
All there for to sleep.

— 14 —

As she stood over Him
She heard Angels sing,
"Oh! bless our dear Saviour,
Our heavenly King."

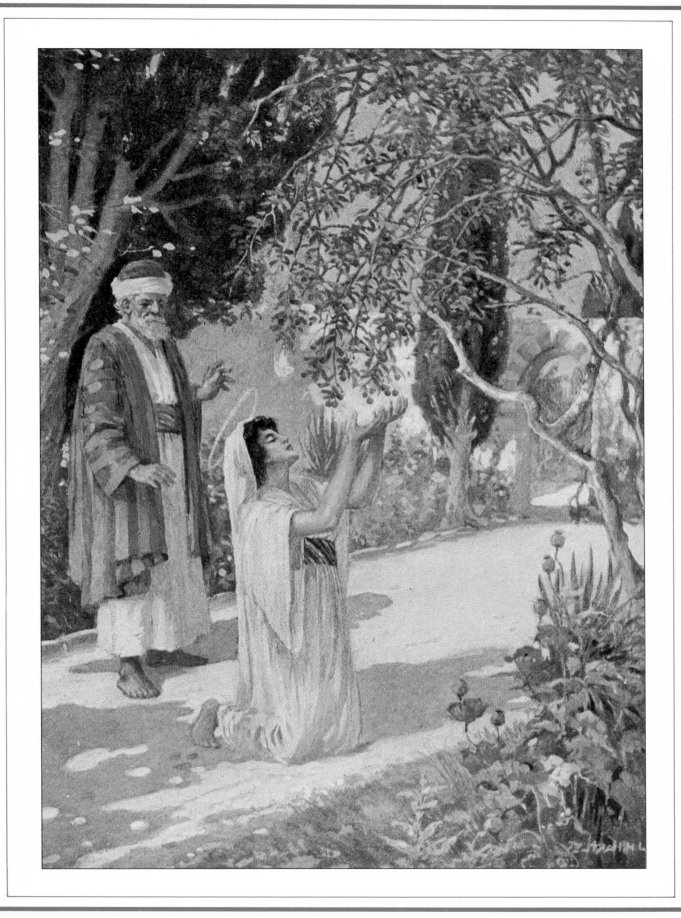

THE HOLLY AND THE IVY

mf
The hol - ly and the i - vy Now both are full well

f
grown, Of all the trees that are in the wood, The

CHORUS.
p
hol - ly bears the crown. O the ri - sing

f
of the sun, The run - ning of the deer, . . The

play - ing of the mer - ry or - gan, Sweet sing - ing in the

quire, . . Sweet sing - ing in the quire. . .

— 2 —

The holly bears a blossom,
As white as lily-flower;
And Mary bore sweet Jesus Christ,
To be our sweet Saviour.
O the rising of the sun, &c.

— 3 —

The holly bears a berry,
As red as any blood;
And Mary bore sweet Jesus Christ,
To do poor sinners good.
O the rising of the sun, &c.

— 4 —

The holly bears a prickle,
As sharp as any thorn;
And Mary bore sweet Jesus Chist,
On Christmas Day in the norm.
O the rising of the sun, &c.

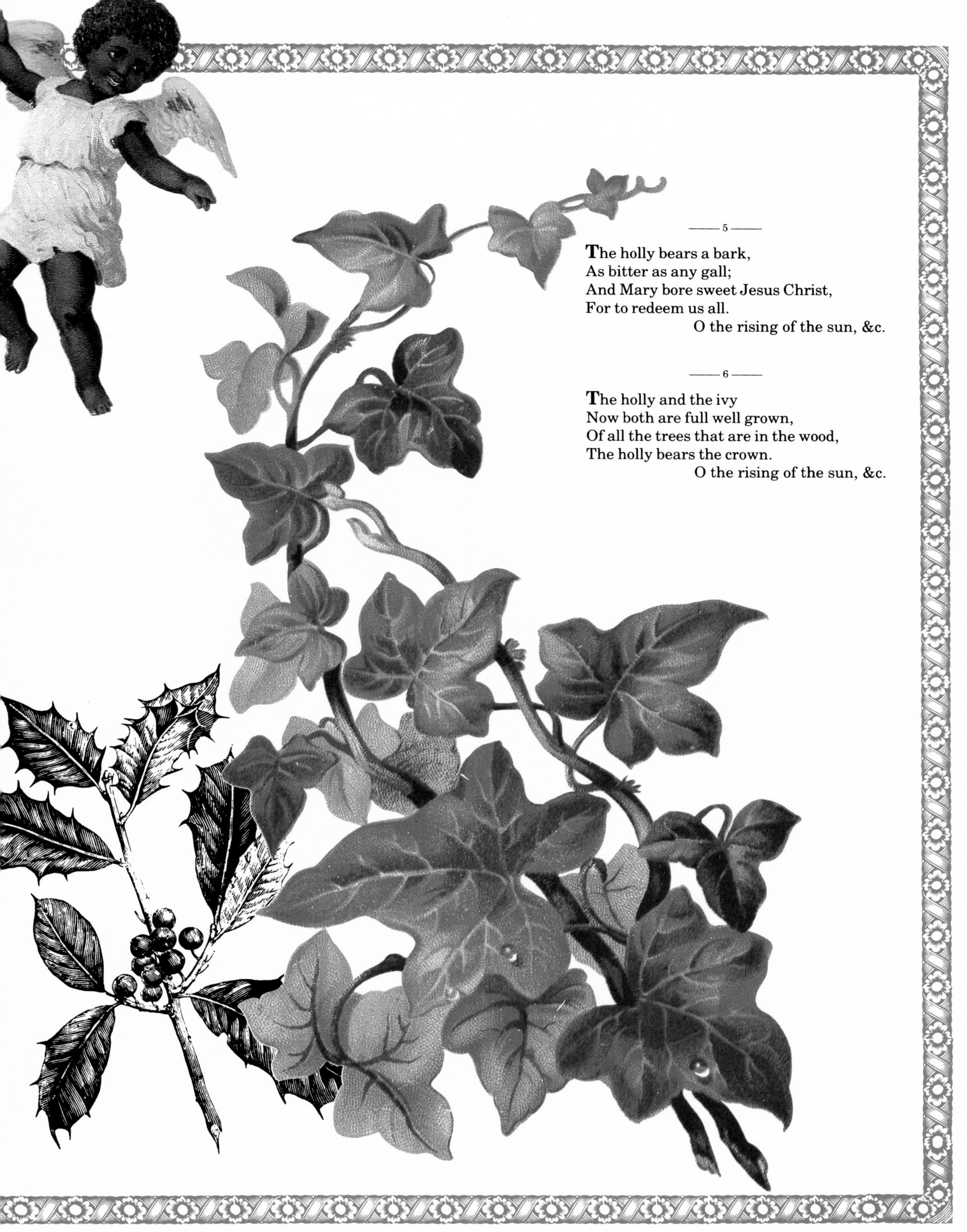

— 5 —

The holly bears a bark,
As bitter as any gall;
And Mary bore sweet Jesus Christ,
For to redeem us all.
O the rising of the sun, &c.

— 6 —

The holly and the ivy
Now both are full well grown,
Of all the trees that are in the wood,
The holly bears the crown.
O the rising of the sun, &c.

WHILE SHEPHERDS WATCHED THEIR FLOCKS

While Shep - herds watched their flocks . . . . by
night, All seat - - ed on the ground,
The An - gel of the LORD came down, The
An - gel of the LORD came down, And
glo - ry shone a - - round, The An - gel of the
LORD came down, And glo - - ry shone a - round.

— 2 —

"Fear not," said he, (for mighty dread
Had seized their troubled mind);
"Glad Tidings of great joy I bring
To you and all mankind.

— 3 —

"To you in David's town this day
Is born, of David's line,
The Saviour, Who is Christ the Lord,
And this shall be the sign.

— 4 —

"The Heavenly Babe you there shall find,
To human view displayed,
All meanly wrapped in swathing bands
And in a Manger laid."

— 5 —

Thus spake the Seraph, and forthwith
Appeared a shining Throng
Of Angels, praising God, and thus
Addressed their joyful song:

— 6 —

"All Glory be to God on High,
And to the earth be Peace;
Goodwill, henceforth, from Heaven to men,
Begin and never cease."

J. H. HARTLEY

DING DONG MERRILY ON HIGH

Ding dong! mer-ri-ly on high in heav'n the bells are ring-ing:

Ding dong! ve-ri-ly the sky is riv'n with An-gel sing-ing.

Glo -

- - - - - - - - - - ri-a, Ho - san-na in ex - cel - sis!

— 2 —

E'en so here below, below,
Let steeple bells be swungen,
And *io, io, io,*
By priest and people sungen.

— 3 —

Pray you, dutifully prime
Your Matin chime, ye ringers;
May you beautifully rime
Your Evetime Song, ye singers:

MI
RE

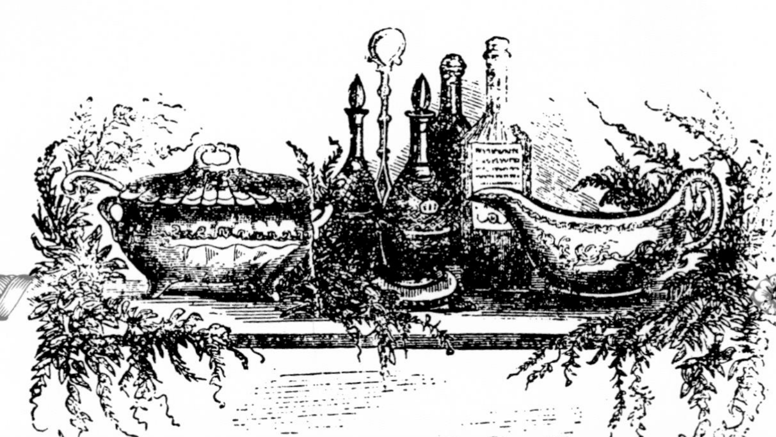